THE HAZARDOUS EARTH

FLOODS

Hazards of Surface and Groundwater Systems

FLOODS

Hazards of Surface and Groundwater Systems

Timothy Kusky, Ph.D.

Facts On File
An imprint of Infobase Publishing

This book commemorates Charlie Belt's pioneering contributions to understanding the hazards of constricting rivers through the construction of levees, the harm that levees cause the natural ecosystems of floodplains, and the hazards levees pose to those whose livelihoods depend on floodplains.

■ ■ ■

FLOODS: Hazards of Surface and Groundwater Systems

Copyright © 2008 by Timothy Kusky, Ph.D.

Facts On File, Inc.
An imprint of Infobase Publishing
132 West 31st Street
New York NY 10001

Library of Congress Cataloging-in-Publication Data

Kusky, Timothy M.
    Floods : hazards of surface and groundwater systems / author, Timothy Kusky.
        p. cm.—(The hazardous Earth)
    Includes bibliographical references and index.
    ISBN-13: 978-0-8160-6468-7
    ISBN-10: 0-8160-6468-7
    1. Floods—Juvenile literature. 2. Groundwater—Pollution—Juvenile literature.
    3. Water—Pollution—Juvenile literature. I. Title.
    GB1399.K87 2008
    551.48'9—dc22   2007051973

Facts On File books are available at special discounts when purchased in bulk quantities for businesses, associations, institutions, or sales promotions. Please call our Special Sales Department in New York at (212) 967-8800 or (800) 322-8755.

You can find Facts On File on the World Wide Web at http://www.factsonfile.com

Text design by Erika K. Arroyo
Illustrations by Richard Garratt
Photo research by Suzanne M. Tibor, Ph.D.

Printed in the United States of America

VB ML 10 9 8 7 6 5 4 3 2 1

This book is printed on acid-free paper and contains 30 percent
  stconsumer reycled content.

Contents

Preface

Natural geologic hazards arise from the interaction of natural Earth processes and humans. Recent natural disasters such as the 2004 Indian Ocean tsunami that killed more than a quarter million people and earthquakes in Iran, Turkey, and Japan have shown how the motion of the Earth's tectonic plates can suddenly make apparently safe environments dangerous or even deadly. The slow sinking of the land surface along many seashores has made many of the world's coastal regions prone to damage by ocean storms, as shown disastrously by Hurricane Katrina in 2005. Other natural Earth hazards arise gradually, such as the migration of poisonous radon gas into people's homes. Knowledge of the Earth's natural hazards can lead one to live a safer life, providing guiding principles on where to build homes, where to travel, and what to do during natural hazard emergencies.

The eight-volume The Hazardous Earth set is intended to provide middle- and high-school readers with a readable yet comprehensive account of natural geologic hazards, the geologic processes that create the hazards to humans, and what can be done to minimize their effects. Titles in the set present clear descriptions of plate tectonics and associated hazards, including earthquakes, volcanic eruptions, landslides, and soil and mineral hazards, as well as hazards resulting from the interaction of the ocean, atmosphere, and land, such as tsunamis, hurricanes, floods, and drought. After providing the reader with an in-depth knowledge of naturally hazardous processes, each volume gives vivid accounts of historic disasters and events that have shaped human history and serve as examples for future generations.

One volume covers the basic principles of plate tectonics and earthquake hazards, and another volume covers hazards associated with volcanoes. A third volume is about tsunamis and related wave phenomena, and another volume covers landslides, soil, and mineral hazards, which includes discussions of mass wasting processes, soils, and the dangers of the natural concentration of hazardous elements such as radon. A fifth volume covers hazards from climate change and drought changing the land surface, and how they affect human populations. This volume also discusses glacial environments and landforms, shifting climates, and desertification, all related to the planet's oscillations back and forth into ice ages and hothouses. Greater understanding is achieved by discussing environments on Earth that resemble icehouse (glaciers) and hothouse (desert) conditions. A sixth volume, entitled *The Coast,* includes discussion of hazards associated with hurricanes, coastal subsidence, and the impact of building along coastlines. A seventh volume, *Floods,* discusses river flooding and flood disasters, as well as many of the contemporary issues associated with the world's diminishing freshwater supply in the face of a growing population. This book also includes a chapter on sinkholes and phenomena related to water overuse. An eighth volume, *Asteroids and Meteorites,* presents information on impacts that have affected the Earth, their effects, and the chances that another impact may occur soon on Earth.

The Hazardous Earth set is intended overall to be a reference book set for middle school, high school, and undergraduate college students, teachers and professors, scientists, librarians, journalists, and anyone who may be looking for information about Earth processes that may be hazardous to humans. The set is well illustrated with photographs and other illustrations, including line art, graphs, and tables. Each volume stands alone and can also be used in sequence with other volumes of the set in a natural hazards or disasters curriculum.

Acknowledgments

Many people have helped me with different aspects of preparing this volume. I would especially like to thank Carolyn, my wife, and my children Shoshana and Daniel for their patience during the long hours spent at my desk preparing this book. Without their understanding this work would not have been possible. Frank Darmstadt, executive editor, reviewed and edited all text and figures, providing guidance and consistency throughout; Suzie Tibor was invaluable as a photo researcher to find high-quality photos for this book. Many sections of the work draw from my own experiences doing scientific research in different parts of the world, and it is not possible to thank the hundreds of colleagues whose collaborations and work I have related in this book. Their contributions to the science that allowed the writing of this volume are greatly appreciated. I wish to thank Louise Belt and family for the generous gift to establish the Belt Laboratory for River and Floodplain Hazards in the New Center for Environmental Sciences at St. Louis University. I have tried to reference the most relevant works or, in some cases, more recent sources that have more extensive reference lists. Any omissions are unintentional.

Introduction

F*loods* are the most common natural hazard, affecting more people and causing more damage than any other hazard, including earthquakes, volcanic eruptions, landslides, and tsunamis. This book describes different types of floods, how normal river systems work and what leads to floods, and what the different types of hazard are to people who are affected by them. There are many different types of floods, ranging from torrents of water that rush out of mountain canyons in dramatic *flash floods,* to slowly rising regional floods that cover wide areas as a result of prolonged and excessive rainfall and snowmelt. Coastal storms such as hurricanes typically push high waters in front of them as they advance, flooding low-lying coastal areas with ocean water. Still other floods result from blocks of ice forming temporary dams along rivers during the time of spring breakup, when the rivers start to thaw and send large pieces of river ice into downstream areas.

Floods have become more of a hazard to people as more and more people have been moving onto *floodplains* and modifying rivers, streams, and the entire floodplain. Many of these modifications to river-floodplain systems were done before the fragile nature of these systems was appreciated and before it was understood that changing part of the system would result in changes to other parts of the system. Human modifications to rivers and floodplains have resulted in more frequent, stronger, faster-moving floods that have done more damage than if the river-floodplain systems were left in their natural states. This book examines historical changes to river systems by people, focusing on the Mississippi-Missouri River system, and examines how modifications to the river system have resulted in progressively more damaging floods over the past 200 years.

This book also describes the change in land use on floodplains with time and how recent changes have led to a loss of fragile ecosystems and increased the risk of flooding to people living on the floodplains. River valley floodplains have been preferred sites for human habitation and farming for millions of years, going back as far as our earliest known ancestors in Turkana Gorge in the Great Rift Valley of Kenya. Stream and river valleys provide routes of easy access through rugged mountainous terrain, and they also provide water for drinking, watering animals, and for irrigation. The soils in river valleys are also some of the most fertile that can be found, as yearly or less frequent floods replenish them. The ancient Egyptians appreciated this, with their entire culture developed in the Nile River Valley revolving around the flooding cycles of the river. Rivers now provide easy and relatively cheap transportation on barges, and the river valleys are heavily used

A woman carries her baby in the flooded Mohammadpur area on the outskirts of Dhaka, Bangladesh, August 12, 2002. *(AP)*

routes for roads and railways as they are relatively flat and easier to build on than mountains. In recent years many floodplains have been so extensively urbanized that their river can no longer migrate across its own floodplain and is confined to a narrow channel. Many surfaces that used to be porous and absorb waters from floods are now covered with pavement, so water from floods cannot sink into the ground. The result is that most of the water must move down the river channel more quickly than in its natural state, resulting in more disastrous floods with increased *urbanization.*

This book describes the science of how and why rivers and floodplains are dynamic environments. Their banks are prone to erosion, and the rivers periodically flood over their banks. During floods rivers typically cover their floodplains with 5–10 feet (1–3 m) of water and drop layers of silt and mud. This is part of a river's normal cycle and was relied upon by the ancient Egyptians for replenishing and fertilizing their fields. In the past century thousands of miles of earthen *levees,* flood walls, and river control structures have been built along many of the nation's and world's rivers, and local legislation allowing extensive development of the floodplains has crept into place in many states. As the floodplains are cordoned off by levees and towns are built on the floodplain, the ability of the floodplain to perform its natural functions decreases. The soils are no longer replenished and fertilized by annual floods, the floodplains can no longer absorb the water from spring floods and reduce the severity of floods, and many critical natural *ecosystems* are threatened. Some species of fish and other fauna and flora that rely on the annual flood cycle on the floodplains have become threatened and may become extinct.

Examples of different flood disasters are described in this book. Many residents of floodplains are living with a false sense of security, since they are told and believe that the levees holding back the rivers are safe and that floods do not threaten their homes and businesses; however, extended floods, such as the 1973 and 1993 floods along the Mississippi River, show that this security is not certain. In the 1993 floods nearly 80 percent of the private levees along the river were overtopped, breached, or failed, causing billions of dollars of damage. Since then many areas on floodplains, such as the Chesterfield Valley along the Missouri River, have seen more development on the floodplain, in areas that were under 5–10 feet (1–3 m) of water in the 1993 floods, than in the entire previous history of the region. Global *climate change* models suggest that the central plains of the United States may enter a much wetter climate phase within the next 30 years, dramatically increasing the frequency and intensity of floods. What used to be the 100-year flood may soon become the seven-year flood.

The water in rivers and streams is part of the *hydrosphere* of the Earth, consisting of all of the water on the planet, including that stored in the *groundwater* system beneath the ground. Of the water in the hydrosphere 97 percent is salt water in the ocean, and of the remaining few percent, only a small fraction of that is available to people for drinking, irrigation, and other uses. This book also examines how people are using this water, and the geological hazards associated with the use and misuse of this water. As the global population increases, water issues will become increasingly important because fewer people will have access to clean water. Many streams and rivers have also become polluted as industry has dumped billions of gallons of chemical waste into

Collecting river water at River Mithi that passes through Mumbai, India, July 4, 2007. The river is a natural drainage channel, carrying excess water during monsoons, but is filthy mainly due to slums and discharge of industrial effluents. *(AP)*

our nation's and the world's waterways. Other pollutants are seeping into water of the groundwater system, ruining this vital resource.

Some people are drinking their demise from water obtained from below the surface. On the Indo-Gangetic plain, south of the Himalaya in India and Bangladesh, many groundwater wells are contaminated with natural arsenic. Between 25 and 75 million people are drinking this water, becoming contaminated, and suffering from the awful effects of arsenic poisoning. Much of this suffering is preventable. It is a simple matter to get water from nearby, uncontaminated wells; however, many of the local people do not understand the danger and cannot afford the energy to walk the extra three miles (5 km) to get the water from a clean well. Monitoring groundwater arsenic levels could prevent much of this poisoning, and this is being done by several United Nations (UN) organizations with limited success. Getting drinking water in many parts of the world is not as simple as turning on the faucet in the United States. Somebody, usually the women, must carry vessels from the home to the well or river, fill the vessels, and carry them back to the home. Some wells are simple and easily accessed; others involve long climbs down treacherous paths in narrow caves that lead to the groundwater level. In many places in the world large parts of the population drink water from polluted rivers, the same rivers that are used for dumping industrial and farm waste, sewage, and anything else washed from the land.

A final subject addressed in this book is ground *subsidence,* which is often caused by the pumping or extraction of groundwater from natural reservoirs below the surface. In some cases this has caused the ground surface to drop several or tens of feet (1–3 m), and in other cases giant sinkholes have suddenly opened, swallowing cars, houses, and disrupting lives of those affected. Extraction of fluids from the subsurface in coastal areas can cause the ground to subside below sea level, leading to the shoreline migrating inland. Pumping of water from coastal wells can also cause the seawater to seep into the wells, ruining them and destroying the aquifer. Issues of groundwater use, pollution, and subsidence are discussed and presented with a review of other mechanisms of ground subsidence so that readers of the book can understand whether the actions of people or natural processes are causing the sinking of the land in specific cases. Examples are presented throughout the text, and possible solutions to difficult problems of water use and misuse are discussed.

This book is organized so that chapter 1 discusses the global distribution and use of water on the planet and how the nations of the world need to address the increasing shortage of clean water as global populations grow exponentially. Chapter 2 discusses the geology and dynamic behavior of different types of stream, river, and floodplain systems. Chapter 3 examines how people's changes to river-floodplain systems, such as the construction of levees and urbanization of the floodplain, have changed the dynamics and behavior of these systems, increasing the risk of more dangerous floods. Chapter 4 presents historical accounts of different types of floods. The last two chapters examine other parts of the hydrosphere, including aspects of the groundwater system and groundwater pollution in chapter 6, and ground subsidence, compaction, and collapse, often associated with groundwater extraction, in chapter 7. A final chapter summarizes and links different chapters in the book.

1

The Water Planet:
Relationships between Surface Water and Groundwater Systems

A view of the planet Earth from space reveals that most of the surface is covered in water, in stark contrast to every other planet. The water on our planet is responsible for many things that allow us to be here. Water lubricates the upper layers of the planet and allows *plate tectonics* to operate, and controls *climate*, weathering, and is part of life itself, found in the bodies of complex fauna and flora to the interior of cells of the most simple single-celled organisms. The surface of the Earth is covered by about 70 percent water, and the bodies of humans are also composed of about 70 percent water.

Water is our most precious resource, needed for sustaining all life, yet has also become our most threatened resource with pollution and overuse. Water can pose risks for catastrophic floods with increased urbanization of areas that used to store water on floodplains. Wars and political battles have been and will be fought over the ability to obtain freshwater, navigate rivers, irrigate farmland, and develop floodplains. Water rights pose difficult political issues in places where it is scarce, such as in the U.S. West and the Middle East. Since we live in a finite world with a finite amount of freshwater and the global population is growing rapidly, it is likely that management of freshwater will become an increasingly important topic for generations to come, yet public and political understanding of the science behind decisions on how to use water lags far behind actual political decision making and land use.

Fresh Groundwater versus Surface Water

Even though most of the surface of the planet is covered with water, more than 97 percent of this water is salty and not readily usable for most purposes to humans. While the oceans may produce enormous amounts of food, offer transportation, and eventually provide a source of energy, humans require freshwater for drinking, agriculture, and industry. Freshwater is becoming the most valuable resource in the world,

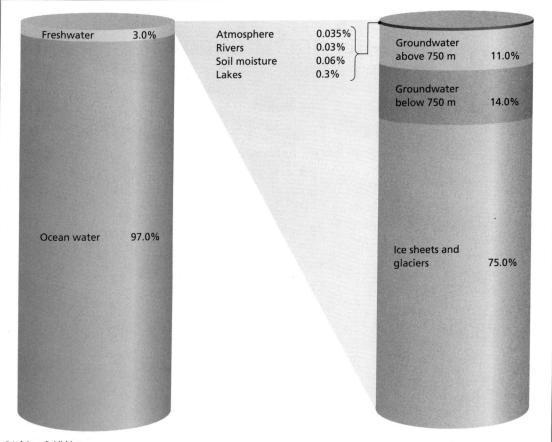

Freshwater	3.0%
Atmosphere	0.035%
Rivers	0.03%
Soil moisture	0.06%
Lakes	0.3%
Groundwater above 750 m	11.0%
Groundwater below 750 m	14.0%
Ocean water	97.0%
Ice sheets and glaciers	75.0%

Bar graphs showing the distribution of water in the hydrosphere. Ninety-seven percent of the planet's water in the hydrosphere is salt water located in the oceans. Three percent of the planet's water is fresh, but 75 percent of that small fraction is locked up in glacial ice. Most of the remaining freshwater is located underground in the groundwater system, and less than one-tenth of the world's freshwater is readily accessible to people in freshwater streams, rivers, and lakes.

and because of the uneven distribution of freshwater in a world with a rapidly growing population, there have been and will be many political debates and outright conflicts over the rights to and use of freshwater. At present people use more than half of all the freshwater that flows in rivers or is stored in lakes, and this percentage is growing rapidly. Other sources of water are being exploited, including extraction from beneath the ground to building reservoirs behind large dam projects.

The volume of groundwater is 35 times the volume of freshwater in lakes and streams, but overall freshwater accounts for less than 3 percent of the planet's water. The United States and other nations have come to realize that freshwater is a vital resource for their survival and are only recently beginning to appreciate that natural and human-aided processes have contaminated much of the world's water resources. Most drinking water in the United States comes from surface reservoirs or is purified from rivers, yet approximately 40 percent of drinking water in the country comes from groundwater reservoirs; about 80 billion gallons of groundwater are pumped out of these reservoirs every day in the United States. Groundwater is a limited resource since it is being pumped out of the ground faster than natural processes are replenishing it.

Water is one of the most unusual substances on the planet and in the entire solar system. Its unusual properties are responsible for controlling climate, life, and many processes on Earth. The water molecule H_2O consists of two hydrogen atoms bonded to one oxygen atom and is a polar molecule with a positive charge at the end with hydrogen and a negative charge at the end containing the oxygen atom. This allows different water molecules to form weak bonds, known as hydrogen bonds, with other water molecules, as the positive end of one molecule will bond with the negative end of an adjacent molecule. The nature of this bond determines the properties of water, such as its melting-freezing point of 32°F (0°C) and boiling point of (212°F (100°C). Water may exist in three different states; as a solid (ice), liquid (water), or vapor (water vapor or steam). Since most of the planet has a temperature between 32 and 212°F (0 and 100°C), most water exists in the liquid form.

One of the most unusual properties of water is that, like other compounds, it contracts and becomes denser as it gets cooler—until about 39°F (4°C), at which point the cold water begins to become less dense again, becoming less dense than the warmer water. This property of water allows ice to float and water bodies to freeze from the top downward. If water were not so unusual, lakes and oceans would freeze from the bottom up and eventually become solid ice. No life would live beneath the seas, and the planet would become a giant cold iceball.

Water can also absorb a lot of heat or solar energy without becoming much warmer. This property is described as having a high *heat capacity,* meaning that large water bodies do not change temperature very rapidly and have a moderating climatic effect on nearby landmasses. It also takes a large amount of energy to change water from a liquid state to a vapor. To change liquid water to vapor the water absorbs a lot of this heat energy from the source (say the ocean) and carries this heat (called the *heat of vaporization*) to the atmosphere, warming the atmosphere. This is one of the most important heat transfer processes on the surface of the planet and plays a large role in many atmospheric and climate effects. The processes can be appreciated on a personal level by feeling the cooling effect of allowing perspiration to evaporate from your body. Water may also sublimate (move directly from the solid to the vapor state) or move from the groundwater system to water vapor in the atmosphere through the aid of *transpiration* in plants.

Water is also able to dissolve many substances with time and can carry many substances in solution. Most water contains many mineral salts (such as sodium chloride, or sea salt) derived from erosion of the landmasses and many dissolved gases from the atmosphere. The amount of gases dissolved in seawater is partly a function of temperature and plays a large role in climate and *global warming.*

The Water Cycle

The water cycle describes the sum of processes operative in the hydrosphere, a dynamic mass of liquid continuously on the move between the different reservoirs on land and in the oceans and atmosphere. The hydrosphere includes all the water in oceans, lakes, streams, glaciers, atmosphere, and groundwater, although most water is in the oceans. The *hydrologic, or water, cycle* describes changes, both long and short term, in the Earth's hydrosphere. It is powered by heat from the Sun, which causes water to change its state through evaporation and transpiration.

The water cycle can be thought of as beginning in the ocean, where energy from the Sun causes surface waters to evaporate, changing from the liquid to the gaseous states. Evaporation takes heat from the ocean and transfers this heat into the atmosphere. It is estimated that about 102 cubic miles (425 km³) of water evaporate from the ocean each year, leaving the salts behind in the ocean. The water vapor then condenses into water droplets in clouds and eventually falls back to the Earth as

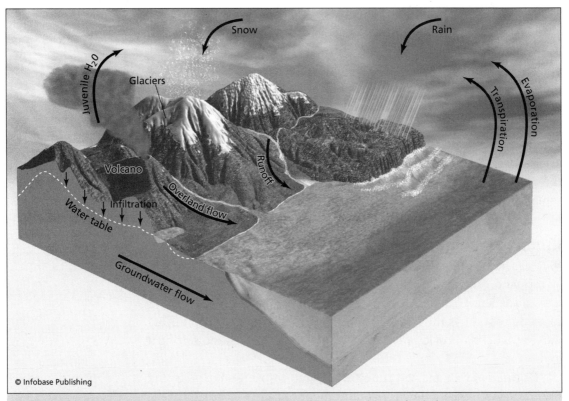

Diagram illustrating the hydrologic cycle. Water evaporates from the oceans and forms clouds that cause precipitation to fall over the land and ocean. The rain and snow that falls on land can run off in rivers to the ocean, seep into the groundwater system, or be used by plants then transpired back to the atmosphere. Water is continuously moving between the different parts of the hydrosphere.

precipitation. Most of the evaporated water, about 92 cubic miles (385 km^3), falls directly back into the ocean, but about 26 cubic miles (111 km^3) of precipitation falls as rain or snow on the continents, transforming the salty water of the oceans into freshwater on land. Nearly three-quarters of this water—17 cubic miles per year (71 km^3/yr)—evaporates back to the atmosphere or is aided by the transpiration from plants, returning the water back to the atmosphere. The other estimated 10 cubic miles (40 km^3) per year of water run across the surface, some of it merging together to form streams and rivers that flow back eventually into the ocean and other parts seeping into the ground to recharge the groundwater system. Humans are now intercepting approximately half of the fresh surface water for drinking, agriculture, and other uses, making a significant impact on the hydrological cycle. Water that seeps into the groundwater system is said to infiltrate, whereas the water that flows across the surface is called *runoff*.

Understanding the water cycle reveals that freshwater is a renewable resource, replenished and cleaned every year, and available for use. However, it must be used wisely, since the quantities are limited, and small amounts of contamination can make entire parts of the system unusable. Freshwater is also supplied unevenly in space and time, with some areas receiving little and other areas receiving freshwater in abundance. The water may come in floods or may be withheld causing drought and suffering. Controlling the flow and usage of freshwater across large regions is one of the major challenges facing humans as the population of the planet grows exponentially and the water supply remains the same.

Running Water as an Erosive Agent

Water is an extremely effective erosional agent, including when it falls as rain and runs across the surface in finger-sized tracks called rivulets and when it runs in organized streams and rivers. Water begins to erode as soon as the raindrops hit the surface: The raindrop impact moves particles of rock, breaking it free from the surface and setting it in motion.

During heavy rains the runoff is divided into *overland flow* and *stream flow.* Overland flow is the movement of runoff in broad sheets. Overland flow usually occurs through short distances before it concentrates into discrete channels as stream flow. Erosion performed by overland flow is known as sheet erosion. Stream flow is the flow of surface water in well-defined channels. Vegetative cover strongly influences the erosive power of overland flow by water. Plants that offer thicker ground cover and have extensive root systems prevent erosion much more than do thin plants and those crops that leave exposed barren soil between rows of crops. Ground cover between that found in true desert and savanna grasslands tends to be eroded the fastest, while tropical rain forests offer the best land cover to protect from erosion. First, the leaves and branches break the force of the falling raindrops, and the roots form an interlocking network that holds soil in place.

Under normal flow regimes, streams attain a kind of equilibrium, eroding material from one bank and depositing on another. Small floods may add material to overbank and floodplain areas, typically depositing layers of silt and mud over wide areas. However, during high-volume floods streams may become highly erosive even removing entire floodplains that may have taken centuries to accumulate. The most severely erosive floods are found in confined channels with high flow, such as where mountain canyons have formed downstream of many small tributaries that have experienced a large rainfall event or in rivers that have been artificially channelized by levees. Other severely erosive floods have resulted from dam failures and in the geological past, about 12,000 years ago, from the release of large volumes of water from ice-dammed lakes. The erosive power of these floodwaters dramatically increases when they reach a velocity known as supercritical flow, at which time they are able to cut through alluvium like butter and even erode bedrock channels. Luckily supercritical flow cannot be sustained for long periods of time, as the effect of increasing the channel size causes the flow to self-regulate and become subcritical.

Cavitation in streams can also cause severe erosion. Cavitation occurs when the stream's velocity is so high that the vapor pressure of water is exceeded and bubbles begin to form on rigid surfaces. These bubbles alternately form and then collapse with tremendous pressure and form an extremely effective erosive agent. Cavitation is visible on some dam spillways, where bubbles form during floods and high *discharge* events, but it is different from the more common and significantly less-erosive phenomena of air entrapment by turbulence, which accounts for most air bubbles observed in white-water streams.

Water as a Resource

Since freshwater is so essential for life, it may be considered an economic resource that needs to be managed effectively for use. Water is needed for drinking, irrigation, household, recreational, and industrial applications. In the United States agriculture uses about 43 percent of all water resources, and industry uses about another 38 percent. On a global scale irrigation for agriculture accounts an even higher percentage of water use, estimated to be 69 percent of total water consumption, whereas industry uses only about 15 percent of water on a global scale. Most of the rest of the water is used by households, for drinking, washing, watering lawns, filling pools, and other benefits of living in a rich society. Americans use an average of 1,585 gallons (6,000 l) of water a day, compared to a bare essential of a half gallon (2 liters) a day needed for survival. Americans use about two to four times as much water as people in western Europe and much more than people in *drought*- and poverty-stricken countries in Africa, and the rest of world.

Water resources are any sources of water that are potentially available for human use, including lakes, rivers, rainfall, reservoirs, and the groundwater system. About two-thirds of the freshwater available on the planet is currently stored in the frozen polar ice caps and in glaciers. Many nations and regions are using the remaining water in streams, lakes, rivers, reservoirs, and in the groundwater system faster than the systems are being replenished by rainfall. Such use is not sustainable, and in time the cost of water will skyrocket, reflecting this supply-and-demand problem. Water use in western European countries is already taxed at much higher rates than in the United States. Taxes may be imposed to help develop more economical sources of water, such as more energy-efficient *desalination* plants along coastal communities.

FAROUK EL-BAZ (1938–): PIONEER IN GROUNDWATER EXPLORATION IN THE SAHARA

Dr. Farouk El-Baz is an Egyptian American well known for pioneering work in the applications of space photography to the understanding of arid terrain, particularly the location of groundwater resources. Based on the analysis of space photographs, his recommendations have resulted in the discovery of groundwater resources in the Sinai Peninsula, the Western Desert of Egypt, and in arid terrains in northern Somalia, the Red Sea Province of Eastern Sudan, Oman, United Arab Emirates, and the Darfur region of Sudan. These discoveries have resulted in many people having the water they need for drinking, agriculture, and development of arid regions. During the past 25 years he contributed to interdisciplinary field investigations in all major deserts of the world, including work in archaeology, geography, and geology.

El-Baz is research professor and director of the Center for Remote Sensing at Boston University. He received a B.Sc. (1958) in chemistry and geology from Ain Shams University in Cairo, Egypt; an M.S. (1961) in geology from the Missouri School of Mines and Metallurgy in Rolla; and a Ph.D. (1964) in geology from the University of Missouri, after performing research at the Massachusetts Institute of Technology (1962–63). He taught geology at Egypt's Assiut University from 1958 to 1960, and at the University of Heidelberg in Germany between 1964 and 1966. In 1989 El-Baz received an honorary Doctor of Science degree from the New England College in Henniker, New Hampshire.

Between 1967 and 1972 El-Baz participated in the Apollo program as supervisor of lunar science planning at Bellcomm, Inc., of Bell Telephone Laboratories in Washington, D.C. During these six years he was secretary of the Site Selection Committee for the Apollo lunar landings, chairman of the Astronaut Training Group, and principal investigator for visual observations and photography. From 1973 to 1983 he established and directed the Center for Earth and Planetary Studies at the National Air and Space Museum of the Smithsonian Institution in Washington, D.C. In 1975 El-Baz was selected by the National Aeronautics and Space Administration (NASA) to be principal investigator for Earth observations and photography on the Apollo-Soyuz Test Project. This was the first joint American-

Water as a Hazard

While the supply of clean freshwater is barely able to meet present demands and is expected to become a larger problem in the future, sometimes there is too much water in one place at one time, creating hazards of another kind. When rains, heavy snowmelts, or combinations of these events bring more water than normal into populated areas, floods result. Many floods cause significant damage and destruction because over the past couple of centuries many cultures have moved large segments of their populations onto floodplains. Floodplains are the flat areas adjacent to rivers that naturally flood, and ancient cultures used these floods and the rich organic mud that covered the floodplains during the floods as natural fertilizers for farmlands. Now that many towns, cities, and population centers have been built on floodplains, people

Soviet space mission. From 1982 to 1986 he was vice president for international development and for science and technology at Itek Optical Systems of Lexington, Massachusetts.

El-Baz served on the Steering Committee of Earth Sciences of the Smithsonian Institution, the Arid and Semi-Arid Research Needs Panel of the National Science Foundation, the Advisory Committee on Extraterrestrial Features of the United States Board of Geographic Names, and the Lunar Nomenclature Group of the International Astronomical Union. In 1979, after the United States and China normalized relations, he coordinated the first visit by U.S. scientists to the desert regions of northwestern China. In 1985 he was elected fellow of the Third World Academy of Sciences and represents the Academy at the Non-Governmental Organizations Unit of the Economic and Social Council of the United Nations. He also served as science adviser (1978–81) to President Anwar el-Sadat of Egypt.

El-Baz is president of the Arab Society of Desert Research and the recipient of numerous honors and awards, including NASA's Apollo Achievement Award, Exceptional Scientific Achievement Medal, and Special Recognition Award; the University of Missouri Alumni Achievement Award for Extraordinary Scientific Accomplishments; the Certificate of Merit of the World Aerospace Education Organization; and the Arab Republic of Egypt Order of Merit—First Class. He also received the 1989 Outstanding Achievement Award of the Egyptian American Organization, the 1991 Golden Door Award of the International Institute of Boston, and the 1992 Award for Public Understanding of Science and Technology of the American Association for the Advancement of Science. In 1995 he received the Award for Outstanding Contributions to Science and Space Technology of the American-Arab Anti-Discrimination Committee and the Achievement Award of the Egyptian American Professional Society, and in 1996, the Michael T. Halbouty Human Needs Award of the American Association of Petroleum Geologists. In 1999 the Geological Society of America established the Farouk El-Baz Award for Desert Research to annually encourage and reward arid land studies.

Floodwaters from the Mississippi River flowing through a town in Missouri during the flood of 1993. Note the wall of sandbags built to try to protect the house from floodwaters. *(Andrea Booher/FEMA)*

regard these natural flood cycles as disasters; in fact, about nine out of every 10 disaster proclamations by the president of the United States is for flood disasters, typically to provide funds to people who have built on floodplains. Additionally, many types of natural vegetation have been removed from hillsides, particularly in urban areas. This reduces the amount of infiltration of water into the hillsides and increases the amount and rate of surface runoff, increasing the danger of floods.

There are many types of floods, including flash floods where huge volumes of water come rushing out of mountain canyons, carrying mud, boulders, and every kind of debris washing into valleys and lowlands. There are floods associated with coastal storms that bring high tides into coastal lowlands and back up river systems across *deltas* and *coastal plains.* Many regions experience slowly rising, long-lasting regional floods associated with spring snowmelts and unusually heavy rains that can last for weeks or months. Some high-latitude climate zones also experience floods in association with the spring breakup of ice on rivers. As the ice melts, blocks move downriver, occasionally getting jammed and forming ice dams, which can cause rapidly rising ice-cold floodwater to cover the river floodplains. These different types of floods, and their causes, are discussed in following chapters.

The World's Diminishing Freshwater Supply with a Growing Population

On a global scale only about half of the world's population has a connection to a piped water supply in their homes, whereas 30 percent rely on wells or local village pipes, and about 20 percent have no access to clean water. The world's population is expected to grow by another 50 percent (another 3–4 billion people) in the next 50 years, so huge investments need to be put into maintaining the existing water supply infrastructure and developing new supply networks. As the population grows and water supplies remain the same or diminish, it is expected that in the next 10 years about half the world's population will not have access to

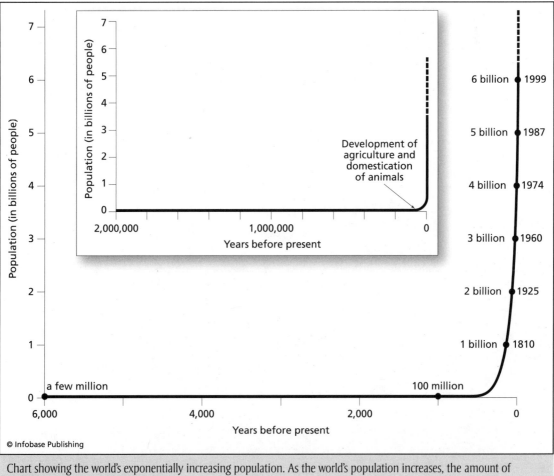

© Infobase Publishing

Chart showing the world's exponentially increasing population. As the world's population increases, the amount of available freshwater remains the same or may be decreasing because of population demands. One of the biggest problems facing the world is how to maintain a clean water supply for a growing population.

clean drinking water. Most of the people without access to clean water for economic reasons are and will be from countries in Africa, South and Central America, and Southeast Asia. Many of the countries of the Middle East face a different problem; a lack of water of any kind. Many of these countries have economic resources and need to start to invest in desalination to meet the needs of their populations.

Presently the highest water consumption per capita is in the United States, followed by rich nations of western Europe. As some developing nations grow in affluence, India and China in particular, the per-capita water use is expected to rise dramatically. With the huge populations of these countries, there will be added stress on the water resources and supply system on a global scale. As populations continue to move into urban areas, countries need to invest in huge water supply and waste-water treatment facilities to ensure clean water for residents. In many places this has meant pumping water out of the ground, but the rate of extraction from groundwater *aquifers* is in many cases faster than the rate at which they are being replenished, so this resource is being depleted.

Global climate change is starting to impact the pattern of global rainfall and water supply. In some places rainfall is expected to diminish, while in other places the amount of rainfall will increase. These

High Bullough Reservoir in Anglezarke Country Park on West Pennine Moors, England *(Alamy)*

Desalination plant in the Caribbean. With continued population growth and a decline in freshwater availability, communities and nations will need to rely more and more on expensive desalination to supply basic water needs. *(Shutterstock)*

changes in climate patterns may dictate massive changes in agricultural patterns and even in population trends within and among nations. It is time that scientists, politicians, and planners all start to discuss how to handle the coming changes on a dynamic planet.

Desalination

Desalination includes a group of water treatment processes that remove salt from water. It is becoming increasingly important as freshwater supplies dwindle and population grows on the planet, yet desalination is exorbitantly expensive and cannot be afforded by many countries. Only 3 percent of the water on the planet is freshwater, and of this, 27 percent is locked up in glaciers, and another 72 percent is groundwater. The remaining 1 percent of the freshwater on Earth is becoming rapidly polluted and unusable for human consumption.

There are a number of different processes that can accomplish desalination of salty water, whether it comes from the oceans or the ground. These are divided broadly into thermal processes, membrane processes, and minor techniques such as freezing, membrane distillation, and solar humidification. All existing desalination technologies require energy input to work and end up separating a clear fraction or stream of water from a stream enriched in concentrated salt that must be disposed of, typically by returning it to the sea.

Thermal distillation processes produce about half of the desalted water in the world. In this process salt water is heated or boiled to produce vapor that is then condensed to collect freshwater. There are many varieties of this technique, including processes that reduce the pressure and boiling temperature of water to effectively cause flash vaporization, using less energy than simply boiling the water. The multistage flash distillation process is the most widely used around the world. In this technique steam is condensed on banks of tubes that carry chemically treated seawater through a series of vessels known as brine heaters with progressively lower pressures, and this freshwater is gathered for use. A technique known as multi-effect distillation has been used for industrial purposes for many years. Multi-effect distillation uses a series of vessels with reduced ambient pressure for condensation and evaporation and operates at lower temperatures than multistage flash distillation. Salt water is generally preheated and then sprayed on hot evaporator tubes to promote rapid boiling and evaporation. The vapor and steam are then collected and condensed on cold surfaces, whereas the concentrated brines are run off. Vapor compression condensation is often used in combination with other processes or by itself for small-scale operations. Water is boiled, and the steam is ejected and mechanically compressed to collect freshwater.

Membrane processes operate on the principle of membranes being able to selectively separate salts from water. Reverse osmosis, commonly used in the United States, is a pressure-driven process in which water is pressed through a membrane, leaving the salts behind. Electrodialysis uses electrical potential, driven by voltage, to selectively move salts through a membrane, leaving freshwater behind. Electrodialysis operates on the principle that most salts are ionic and carry an electrical charge, so they can be driven to migrate toward electrodes with the opposite charge. Membranes are built that allow passage of only certain types of ions, typically either positively (cation) or negatively (anion) charged. Direct current sources with positive and negative charges are placed on either side of the vessel, with a series of alternate cation and anion selective membranes placed in the vessel. Salty water is pumped through the vessel, the salt ions migrate through the membranes to the pole with the opposite charge, and freshwater is gathered from the other end of the vessel. Reverse osmosis only appeared technologically feasible in the 1970s. The main energy required for this process is for applying the pressure to force the water through the membrane. The salty feed water is preprocessed to remove suspended solids and chemically treated to prevent microbial growth and precipitation. As the water is forced through the membrane, a portion of the salty feed water must be discharged from the process to prevent the precipitation of super-saturated salts. Presently membranes are made of hollow fibers or spiral wound. Improvements in energy recovery and membrane technology have decreased the cost of reverse osmosis, and this trend may continue, particularly with the use of new nanofiltration membranes that can soften water in the filtration process by selectively removing calcium and magnesium ions.

Several other processes have been less successful in desalination. These include freezing, which naturally excludes salts from the ice crystals. Membrane distillation uses a combination of membrane and distillation processes, which can operate at low temperature differentials but require large fluxes of salt water. Solar humidification was used in World War II for desalination stills in life rafts, but these are not particularly efficient because they require large solar collection areas, have a high capital cost, and are vulnerable to weather-related damage.

Conclusion

Water covers about 70 percent of the surface of the Earth, yet less than 1 percent of this is freshwater available for human consumption. The water moves around the planet in the water or hydrologic cycle, evaporating from the oceans and forming clouds in the sky that cause precipitation on the land and oceans. Water, snow, and ice that fall on the land either run off in streams and rivers, evaporate, are used and transpired by plants, or seep into the groundwater system. There is about 35 times as much water in the groundwater system as in surface reservoirs, yet presently 20 percent of the world's population has no access to clean water, and half of the world's population does not have piped water in their homes. This situation is getting worse as the world's population increases rapidly and as surface and groundwater supplies are used up and become polluted or contaminated.

Water can also be a problem in situations where there is too much of it at one time in one place. Floods occur when rivers flow out of their banks onto floodplains, covering wide flat areas with several feet of water and depositing thin layers of mud and silt. Ancient civilizations used the flooding cycles of rivers to fertilize agricultural fields, but modern societies have placed cities and towns on floodplains, where it becomes necessary to build extensive flood control measures. When these fail floods become disasters, lives are lost, and great property damage occurs. Nine out of 10 disaster declarations in the United States are for flooding events like this, and the most deadly natural disasters of all time have been cases where rivers, particularly the Yellow River of China, have flowed out of their channels covering vast floodplains with water and killing many hundreds of thousands, and even millions, of people. Clearly nations need to rethink the trend of developing flood-plains for uses other than agriculture.

Global climate change is starting to impact the pattern of rainfall and river flow on a global scale, and many climate belts are migrating. Local patterns of climate and precipitation change should be understood to know how best to deal with climate change.

2

Streams and River Systems

Rivers are the main geological instruments that shape the surface of the land, carrying pieces of the continents grain by grain, steadily to the sea. They slowly erode mountains and fill deep valleys with alluvium, and serve as passageways for people, aquatic fauna and flora, sediment, and dissolved elements from one place to another. River systems are not simply a channel but are intricately linked to associated floodplains and deltas and are affected by processes that occur throughout the entire drainage basin. Rivers transport water in a critical step in the hydrological cycle and bring freshwater to even the driest places on Earth. Nearly every city and town in the world is built with a river flowing through it or near it, so vital is water for drinking, agriculture, and navigation. Rivers have controlled history, bringing life to some areas, but also are prone to floods, sometimes bringing disaster from the same source that has fed populations for ages.

In this chapter the geometry of streams and channel patterns are described, and the processes that control whether a river is straight, meanders, or consists of a series of interconnected channels are examined. The physical principles of how a river works and transports sediment are discussed, then different depositional forms, such as deltas, are examined. Finally, different styles and geometries of river networks in an entire drainage basin are described, and the physical factors that determine the style of the river network are examined.

Geometry of Streams

Streams are dynamic, ever-changing systems that represent a balance between driving and resisting forces. The ability of a stream to erode and transport sediments depends on how much energy is in the water as it flows versus how much is consumed by the resistance to flow. As the velocity of the water in the stream increases, the resistance to flow provided by the stream banks, boulders, and material carried by the stream also increases. Therefore, at any point in the stream the velocity of the water and the shape of the stream channel represent a balance between the energy causing the flow of water and the energy consumed by resistance to flow.

The water in the stream channel may exhibit one of two main types of flow, laminar or turbulent. In a *laminar flow* pattern the paths of water particles are parallel and smooth, and the flow is not very erosive.

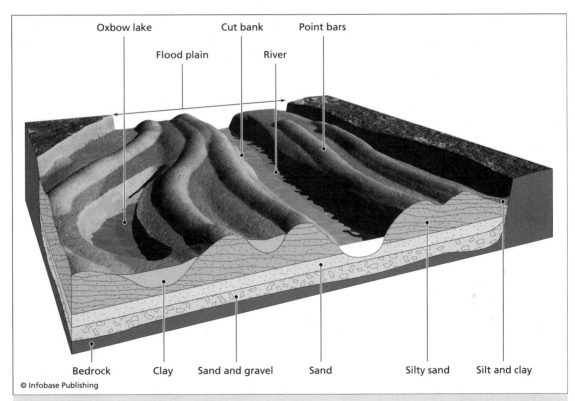

Oxbow lake   Cut bank   Point bars   Flood plain   River

Bedrock   Clay   Sand and gravel   Sand   Silty sand   Silt and clay

© Infobase Publishing

Diagram showing a river flowing through its floodplain. Note how the river channel is asymmetric, deep on one side (cut bank), where the bank may be eroded, and shallow on the other side, where sediments may be deposited on point bars. Rivers tend to migrate back and forth across their floodplains, leaving old river channels behind as oxbow lakes and as buried lenses of clay and sand.

Resistance to flow in laminar systems is provided by internal friction between individual water molecules, and the resistance is proportional to flow velocity. The frictional resistance in laminar flow systems increases from the top of the water surface to the base of the streambed. In contrast, in *turbulent flow* the flow directions and velocity vary in all directions within the stream, and water is being continuously exchanged between adjacent flow zones. In turbulent flows the water may move in different directions and often forms zones of sideways or short backward flows called eddies. These significantly increase the resistance to flow. In turbulent flows the resistance is proportional to the square of the flow velocity. Many zones of turbulence and turbulent eddies are generated along channel margins where the water velocity is reduced by frictional resistance from the bed material and banks of the river.

Streams are defined primarily by their channels, which are the elongate depressions where the water flows. There are several different types of stream banks, which separate the stream channels from the adjacent flat floodplains. The shape of the channel and its pattern in map view represents the balance between the driving and resisting forces in the different conditions or environments through which the stream passes. Streams create their broad flat floodplains by erosion and redeposition during floods, and these plains serve as the stream bottom during large floods. Even though floodplains may not have any water over them for many tens of years, they are part of the stream system, and the stream will return. Many communities in the United States and elsewhere have built extensively on the floodplains, and these communities will eventually be flooded.

Stream channels are self-adjusting features, which modify their shapes and sizes to best accommodate the amount of water flowing in the stream. A stream's discharge is a measure of the amount of water passing a given point per unit time. During floods the discharge may be two, three, 10, or more times normal levels. The stream channel may then overflow, causing the water to spread across the adjacent floodplain, inundating any towns or farms built on the floodplain.

The cross-sectional shape of streams changes with time and amount of water flow through the channel. The shape of a stream channel will also be different in the upstream and downstream parts of the system, as the slope and volume of water changes along the course of the river. Small narrow streams are typically as deep as they are wide, whereas large streams and rivers are much wider than they are deep.

The *gradient,* or slope, of a stream is a measure of the vertical drop over a given horizontal distance, and the average gradient decreases downstream. Going downstream, several changes also occur. First, the discharge increases, which in turn causes the width and depth of the channel to increase. Less intuitively, moving downstream as the gradient decreases, the velocity increases. Although one might expect the velocity of a stream to decrease with a decrease in slope (gradient), anyone who has seen the Mississippi at New Orleans or the Nile at Cairo can testify to their great velocity as compared to their upstream sources. There are two reasons for this increase in velocity. First, the upstream portions of these mighty rivers have courses with many obstacles and more friction per stream volume, reducing velocity. Second, there is more water flowing in the downstream portions of the streams, and this has to move quickly to allow the added discharge from the various tributaries that merge with the main stream.

The base level of a stream is the limiting level below which a stream cannot erode the land. The ultimate base level is sea level, but in many cases streams entering a lake or dammed region form a local base level.

Stream Load

Most energy in streams is dissipated by turbulent flow, but a small part of a stream's energy is used to erode and transport sediments downstream. Streams carry a variety of materials as they make their way to the sea, and the way this material is eroded and transported is dependent on the energy balance in the stream. These materials range from minute dissolved particles and pollutants, to giant boulders moved only during the most massive floods. The *bed load* consists of the coarse particles that move along or close to the bottom of the stream bed. Particles move more slowly than the stream, by rolling, bouncing, or sliding. *Saltation* is the movement of a particle by short intermittent jumps caused by the current lifting the particles. Bed load typically constitutes between 5 and 50 percent of the total load carried by the stream, with a greater proportion carried during high-discharge floods. The *suspended load* consists of the fine particles suspended in the stream. These make many streams muddy, and it consists of silt and clay that moves at the same or slightly lower velocity as the stream. The suspended load generally accounts for 50–90 percent of the total load carried by the stream. The *dissolved load* of a stream consists of dissolved chemicals, such as bicarbonate, calcium, sulfate, chloride, sodium, magnesium, and potassium.

The dissolved load tends to be high in streams fed by groundwater. Pollutants such as fertilizers and pesticides from agriculture and industrial chemicals also tend to be carried as dissolved load in streams.

Most of the larger particles in streambeds are not usually moving, but only move for short distance at times of high-flow velocity and discharge of the stream. The picking up of particles from the bed load of a stream and the erosion of material from the banks is known as *entrainment,* which depends on the erosive power of the flow and the resistance of the particles. There is a wide range in the sizes and amounts of material that can be entrained and transported by a stream. The *competence* of a stream refers to the maximum size of particles that can be entrained and transported by a stream under a given set of hydraulic conditions, measured in diameter of largest bed load. A stream's *capacity* is the potential load it can carry, measured in the amount (volume) of sediment passing a given point in a set amount of time. The amount of material carried by streams depends on a number of factors. Climate studies show erosion rates are greatest in climates between a true desert and grasslands. Topography affects stream load as rugged topography contributes more detritus, and some rocks are more erodable. Human activity such as farming, deforestation, and urbanization strongly affect erosion rates and stream transport. Deforestation and farming greatly increase erosion rates and supply more sediment to streams, increasing their loads. Urbanization has complex effects, including decreased infiltration and decreased times between rainfall events and floods, as discussed in detail below.

Erosion and Deposition along Stream Banks

The process of entrainment determines how a stream erodes its bank and bed and the type of sedimentary load the stream can carry. The lateral, or sideways, erosion of a stream bank is an important process that strongly influences other stream processes. The erosion of the stream banks is accomplished through a combination of processes, including weathering of the material on the stream bank; *mass wasting,* which may cause the bank to collapse into the stream; and the actual entrainment of the sedimentary particles into the bed load of the stream.

The weathering of the bank material, which is typically loose sediments deposited by the stream, makes it weaker and more susceptible to mass movement and collapse into the river. The amount of moisture in the soil on the banks is important in this stage, as increased moisture, as during rain or flooding events, decreases the frictional resistance between the bank sediments, and that is partly why many banks collapse during rains and flooding events. In areas prone to freeze-thaw cycles, stream banks also are susceptible to collapse from the action of frost wedging in small cracks, pushing blocks of sediment into the river. Many stream banks have layers of sand, gravel, and mud deposited on floodplains during earlier stages of the stream development. In these cases groundwater may move along the gravel and sand layers, seeping out along the riverbank. This movement of groundwater can actually carry sediment away from the bank into the stream, in a process called *sapping.* This groundwater sapping creates overhanging banks along the river, which are then prone to collapse. The water along these layers may also reduce the friction on this layer, creating a plane that overlying layers often slide into the river along, forming planar *slides.* Planar slides are recognized as important mass-wasting processes along many riverbanks, including the Mississippi River.

River- and stream banks collapse with many different styles of mass wasting, including slipping of large sections of the bank on rotational slides, *slumps* into the river, and wholesale collapse of large slabs, especially where the stream has undercut the riverbank. Many factors determine which style of collapse occurs, including the layering in the riverbank/floodplain sediment, the pore fluid pressure, the type of material, and the slope.

After the bank materials collapse into the river, the current begins to entrain the finer grained particles and to move the coarser material as bed load. This carries the material away and prepares the bank for the next failure in the steady process of the river migrating across the floodplain.

After the sediments are carried away by the river current, they are at some point deposited again. Fine particles may be carried in suspension all the way to the ocean or local reservoir, whereas most of the coarser particles move by bouncing or rolling along the streambed. Where these sediments get deposited next depends on the interactions of the type of current in the river and the size, shape, and density of the sedimentary particles. The river channel is a very dynamic environment, and the flow velocity and style, whether laminar or turbulent, can vary significantly over short distances. These local variations often determine where a sedimentary particle will be deposited and whether the current is scouring one place or filling in another. Typically, as the river is eroding a bank or scouring its base in one location, moving the material from that location downstream, the current is at the same time depositing other sedimentary material nearby that was carried from farther upstream. For instance, along one bend of a river, the outer or cut bank may be eroding, whereas the inner bank of the bend may be experiencing deposition. In this way the river is able to effectively move its location, filling in the old channel as it cuts a new one, step by step. River floodplains are naturally very dynamic environments where the natural forces in the river keep a balance by maintaining this lateral, back-and-forth type of movement of the channel, as the river transports the bed and suspended load downstream.

If the river cannot move laterally, such as if confined by bedrock or by artificial levees, the river must respond by changing the level of its base. Rivers may downcut through alluvium or bedrock in response to tectonic uplift or may rise through depositing sediments along their beds, in a process called *aggradation*. If the river is transporting a large bed load, it naturally responds to this by moving it downstream and moving sideways. When the bank is confined, it can only move upward and deposits these extra bedload sediments along its base, causing unnatural aggradation.

Channel Patterns

River channels represent a quasi-equilibrium condition between the river discharge, flow regime (whether laminar or turbulent), the amount of sediment being transported, and the slope of the river channel. The river can respond to these variables by finding an equilibrium or quasi-equilibrium condition by adjusting the channel shape (width and depth), the velocity of the flow, the roughness of the bed and bank, and the slope of the bed. The slope of a riverbed can be adjusted by the river by increasing or decreasing the number of bends, or *meanders*, in the river. If the river needs to lower the slope to maintain a quasi-equilibrium condition, then it can increase the number of bends and flow more parallel to the contours. If the river needs to increase the slope, it can cut through the banks and flow straight downhill, attaining a slope equal to the regional gradient. This is one of the reasons rivers have so many different forms, from straight to wildly meandering channels.

STRAIGHT CHANNELS

Stream channels are rarely straight, and a stream is said to have a straight channel if the ratio of the stream length to valley length is 1:5. This ratio is called the *sinuosity*, and although it seems to have no particular mechanical significance, this measure is useful to describe the shape of stream

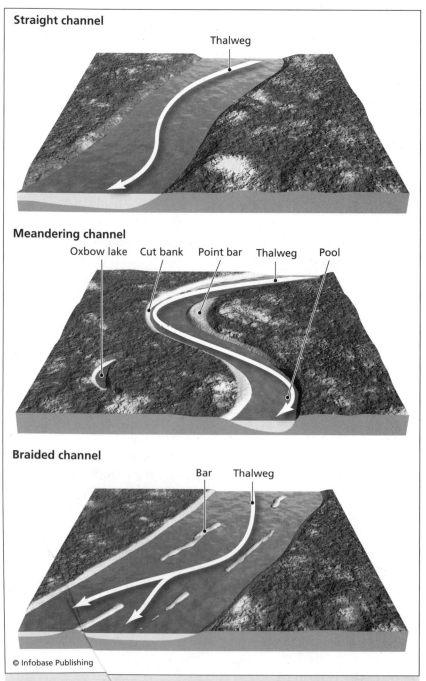

Straight channel

Thalweg

Meandering channel

Oxbow lake   Cut bank   Point bar   Thalweg   Pool

Braided channel

Bar   Thalweg

© Infobase Publishing

Channel patterns of straight, meandering, and braided streams. The heavy white line shows the path of the thalweg, the line connecting the deepest and fastest moving flow in the channel. The patterned areas represent sand and gravel deposited on sandbars and point bars.

A relatively straight stream channel segment along the Rio Grande National Wild and Scenic River as viewed from Santa Elena Canyon area. Mexico is on the left side, and the United States, on the right, specifically Big Bend Park, Texas. *(Photo Researchers, Inc.)*

channels. Many straight stream channels are so because they inherit their path from incision into an underlying bedrock fracture, whereas others are relatively straight for short distances. In either case the velocity of flow changes in different places, and internally the water in the channel naturally starts to develop some complex flow patterns. Friction makes the flow slower on the bottom and sides of the channel, and the water develops curving traces of highest velocity in plan view, and also begins to circulate in loops from the surface, to the streambed, and back to the surface as the water moves downstream. The changing currents cause sandbars to be deposited alternately on either side of the straight channel and for deep pools to develop between the bars. These internal bends in the river make the zone of fastest flow swing from side to side.

Straight channels are very rare, and those that do occur have many properties of curving streams. The *thalweg* is a line connecting the deepest parts of the channel. In straight segments the thalweg typically meanders from side to side of the stream. In places where the thalweg is on one side of the channel, a bar may form on the other side. A bar (for example, a sandbar) is a deposit of alluvium in a stream.

MEANDERING STREAMS

Most streams move through a series of bends known as meanders. The main components of meandering channels are similar to the straight

Meanders and an oxbow lake on the floodplain of the Okavango River, Botswana *(Photo Researchers, Inc.)*

channels, with greater curvature. The outer bends of meanders are typically marked by steep cut banks, with active slumping and mass wasting into the channel, whereas the inner bends of the meanders are marked by deposition of sand and gravel. Meanders are always migrating across the floodplain by the process of the deposition of *point bars* and the erosion of the bank on the opposite side of the stream with the fastest flow. The thalweg, the line of fastest flow, bounces into the outer cut bank, and some of the flow moves down along this steep wall, then more slowly upward along the slope of the point bar as the water moves downstream. This results in a twisting helical flow of water in the stream channel and serves to keep the outer banks erosive, with the fastest currents and the inner point bars have slower velocity currents and receive deposits of sand and gravel. Meanders typically migrate back and forth and also down valley at a slow rate. If the downstream portion of a meander encounters a slowly erodible rock, the upstream part may catch up and cut off the meander. This forms an *oxbow lake,* which is an elongate and curved lake formed from the former stream channel.

Studies on the mechanics of stream flow have revealed that there are quantitative relationships between the wavelength of a meander (the distance from one cut bank to the next one of similar curvature),

A braided stream in Lower Matukituki Valley, New Zealand, looking northwest from Lake Wanaka toward the Harris Mountains in Central Otago, South Island. Note that few channels are active, and there is more sediment in the river than it can transport with current discharge. *(Photo Researchers, Inc.)*

the discharge of the stream, the radius of curvature, and other stream parameters. By changing any of these variables the current in the stream will change to attempt to restore the system to an equilibrium state. Therefore, it is clear that streams need to be able to maintain their migrating meandering pattern across floodplains to be in equilibrium. Any unnatural changes, such as straightening or narrowing channels, will naturally be met by the river with changes in other parameters, that may be unexpected and potentially hazardous.

BRAIDED STREAM CHANNELS

Braided streams consist of two or more adjacent but interconnected channels separated by bars or islands, commonly known as *braid bars*. Braided streams have constantly shifting channels, which move as the bars are eroded and redeposited, during large fluctuations in discharge. Most braided streams have highly variable discharge in different seasons, and they carry more load than meandering streams.

Braided streams tend to be wider and shallower and have steeper gradients than streams with undivided channels. Several factors seem to play significant roles in determining if a stream channel becomes braided. First, the backs of the stream must be easily erodible, letting the channels migrate and contributing bed load to the channel. Second, the load must be large, as all braided streams carry high sediment loads. Third, braided streams are characterized by rapid changes in discharge. Braided streams are common in areas such as on glacial outwash plains, where the fluctuation in discharge is large, there is abundant sediment supply, and the riverbanks are easily erodible.

Dynamics of Stream Flow

Streams are very dynamic systems and constantly change their channel patterns and the amount of water (discharge) and sediment being transported in the system; for example, streams may transport more water and sediment in times of spring floods than in low-flow times of winter or drought. Since streams are dynamic systems, as the amount of water flowing through the channel changes, the channel responds by changing its size and shape to accommodate the extra flow. For instance, in a gradually changing climate scenario, the discharge and load of a river may gradually change, and the river may be able to make small changes accordingly to account for these variables. At some point, however, the balance of controlling forces in the river may exceed a critical threshold value, and the channel may suddenly make a dramatic change into a completely different configuration. In another scenario a river may gradually downcut its gradient through a mountain range, starting as a juvenile high-gradient stream, and over the course of many years gradually decrease its gradient (slope) as the bed is eroded. At different stages in this evolution the stream may make transitions, perhaps rapidly, through different channel types and flow regimes.

The following five factors control how a stream behaves:

1. Width and depth of channel, measured in feet (meters)
2. Gradient, measured as change in elevation in feet per mile (m/km)
3. Average velocity, measured in feet per second (m/sec)
4. Discharge, measured in cubic feet per second (m³/sec)
5. Load, measured as tons per cubic yard (metric tons/m³)

All these factors are continually interplaying to determine how a stream system behaves. As one factor, such as discharge changes, so do the others, expressed as the following:

$$Q = w \times d \times v$$

Other, less important factors may also play a role. These include the mean annual flood, meander wavelength, width-depth ratio, and sinuosity. These secondary variables are not totally independent, as for instance, sinuosity and gradient are related, the mean annual flood and discharge are related, and so on. The main point is that the variables are all interrelated, and changing one can lead to changes in the others.

All factors vary across the stream, so they are expressed as averages. If one term changes then all or one of the others must change too. For example, with increased discharge, the stream erodes and widens and deepens its channel. With increased discharge the stream may also respond by increasing its sinuosity through the development of meanders, effectively creating more space for the water to flow in and occupy

Mountains and a gravel bar along a glacial stream in Northwestern Lagoon, Harris Bay, Kenai Fjords National Park, Alaska. The gravels were deposited where the stream enters the lagoon and the current velocity drops. *(Minden)*

by adding length to the stream. The meanders may develop quickly during floods because the increased stream velocity adds more energy to the stream system, and this can rapidly erode the cut banks, enhancing the meanders.

The amount of sediment load available to the stream is also independent of the stream's discharge, so different types of stream channels develop in response to different amounts of sediment load availability. If the sediment load is low, streams tend to have simple channels, whereas braided stream channels develop where the sediment load is greater. If a large amount of sediment is dumped into a stream, the stream will respond by straightening, thus increasing the gradient and stream velocity and increasing the stream's ability to remove the added sediment.

When streams enter lakes or reservoirs along their path to the sea, the velocity of the stream will suddenly decrease. This causes the sediment load of the stream or river to be dropped as a delta on the lake bottom, and the stream attempts in this way to fill the entire lake with sediment. The stream is effectively attempting to regain its gradient by filling the lake, then eroding the dam or ridge that created the lake in the first place. When the water of the stream flows over the dam, it does so without its sediment load and therefore has greater erosive power and can erode the dam more effectively.

The concept of a *graded stream* is widely used by geomorphologists to describe how a river may adjust its environment to transport its sedimentary load with the least energy required. In this concept the stream gradually, over many years, erodes its bed to attain an equilibrium gradient that is just right for transporting the sedimentary load when balanced with the types of channel characteristics and velocity available in the area. This graded profile is typically concave up, steeper in the headwaters, and with a low slope near the mouth of the river. Graded streams are thought to be in a state of relative equilibrium; changes in

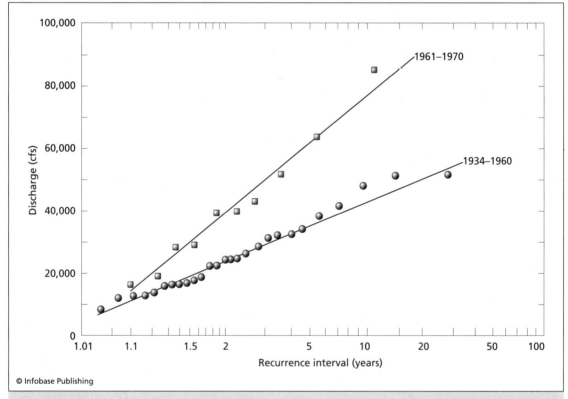

© Infobase Publishing

Flood frequency curve for two different periods of different climates along a river in Africa. The recurrence time (horizontal axis) represents how often a flood with a specific volume of water (vertical axis, showing discharge in cubic feet per second) would occur. Note that the river had a dry climate from 1934 to 1960, and floods were not as large or as frequent as in the wetter time period from 1961 to 1970. Changes in climate can severely impact the predicted frequency of floods. *(Data from the Ministry of Water Development, Kenya)*

one variable will be accommodated by changes in the other to keep the balance of forces.

Floods

Seasonal variations in rainfall cause stream discharge to rise and sometimes overflow the stream's banks. Both stream discharge and velocity increase during floods, so during floods the streams carry larger particles. Many of the most dramatic changes to river channels occur during floods: Meander channels may be cut off, new channels may form, natural levees may be breached, and occasionally, the river may abandon one channel altogether in favor of another. Floods of specific magnitude have a probable interval of recurrence. Small floods occur quite often, typically every year. Larger floods occur less frequently, and the largest floods occur with the longest time interval in between. The time interval between floods of a specific discharge is known as the *recurrence interval,* and this is commonly cited using statistics for the 50-year flood, 100-year flood, 500-year flood, and so on.

Curves of the discharge versus recurrence interval can be drawn for every stream and river to determine its characteristic flooding frequency. This is important information for everyone living near a stream or on a river floodplain to know how likely it is that a flood of a certain height will occur again within a certain time frame. For instance, if a flood of 150 cubic feet/second (4.25 m³/sec) covered a small town with 10 feet of water 30 years ago, is it safe to build a new housing development on the floodplain on the outskirts of town? Using the flood frequency curve for that river, planners could determine that floods of 150 cubic feet/second are expected on average every 40 years, and floods of two times that magnitude are expected every 100 years. Planners and insurers might (in the best of situations) conclude from that information that it is unwise to build extensively on the floodplain and that the new community should be located on higher ground.

Understanding flood frequency and the chances of floods of specific magnitude occurring along a river is also essential for planning many other human activities. It is necessary to know how much water the bridges and drainage pipes must be built to handle and to know how to plan for land use across the floodplain. In many cases bigger, more expensive bridges should be built, even if it seems unlikely that a small stream will ever rise high enough to justify such a high bridge. In other cases structures are built with a short lifetime of use expected, and planners must calculate whether the likelihood of flood warrants the extra cost of building a flood-resistant structure.

WILL CLIMATE CHANGE AFFECT THE RIVER SYSTEMS IN THE UNITED STATES?

The global climate changes on many different time scales, with natural climate changes caused by variations in the amount of incoming solar radiation in cycles of 100,000, 41,000, 23,000, and 11,000 years. It is clear that human activities are also changing the global climate, primarily through the introduction of *greenhouse gases* such as CO_2 into the atmosphere, while cutting down tropical rain forests that act as sinks for the CO_2 and put oxygen back into the atmosphere. The time scale of observation of these human, or *anthropogenic,* changes is short, but the effect is clear, with a nearly 2°F (1°C) change in global temperature measured for the past few decades. The increase in temperature will lead to more water vapor in the atmosphere, and since water vapor is also a greenhouse gas, this will lead to a further increase in temperature. Many computer-based climate models are attempting to predict how much global temperatures will rise as a consequence of human influences, and what effects this temperature rise will have on melting of the ice sheets (which could be catastrophic), sea level rise (perhaps several tens of feet or more), and runaway greenhouse temperature rise (which is possible).

Climate changes are difficult to measure, partly because the instrumental and observational records go back only a couple of hundred years in Europe. From these records global temperatures have risen by about 2°F (1°C) since 1890, most notably between 1890 and 1940 and again since 1970. This variation, however, is small compared to some of the other variations induced by natural causes, and some scientists argue that it is difficult to separate anthropogenic effects from the background natural variations. Rainfall patterns have also changed in the past 50 years, with declining rainfall totals over low latitudes in the Northern Hemisphere, especially in the Sahel, which has experienced major droughts and famine. However, high-latitude precipitation has increased in the same time period. These patterns all relate to a general warming and shifting of the global climate zones to the north.

Research by atmospheric scientist Zaito Pan's group at Saint Louis University has shown that global warming has many regional variations, and some regions known as warming holes will actually become wetter and slightly colder than at present. In the United States the central plains centered on the Missouri River Basin represent a warming hole, formed by the interaction between the convergence of water vapor leading to increased rainfall, accumulation of water in thick soils, and evaporation, which enhances cooling. Other warming holes are centered on the Yellow River Basin of eastern China and the Amazon Basin of South America.

The increased precipitation in these basins is significant and could have major consequence for future floods in these regions; for instance, a predicted 21 percent increase in precipitation for the Missouri-Mississippi River Basins is predicted by the year 2050, along with an alarming 51 percent increase in the amount of water flowing through these rivers. River flood stages will be higher, floods will be more frequent and potentially devastating. The consequences of these climate changes need to be appreciated and prepared for by the people who live in these regions, as well as by developers, insurance underwriters, urban planners, politicians, and the federal government.

Depositional Features: Floodplains, Terraces, and Deltas

During great floods streams flow way out of their banks and fill the adjacent floodplain. During these times, when the water flows out of the channel, its velocity suddenly decreases, and it drops its load, forming levees, and overbank silt deposits on the floodplain.

FLOODPLAINS

Floodplains are relatively flat areas that occupy valley bottoms and are generally made up of unconsolidated sediments. Most of these sediments are deposited by the river, but some may come from other processes, such as from slopes along the margins of the valley or even from wind. In natural river systems (ones not disturbed by levees, etc.), the river will periodically rise out of its banks and cover the floodplain with water and fine sediments. Different flood levels and different parts of the floodplain may be reached with different frequencies of floods. In most natural rivers in humid climates the river rises out of the banks every year or two. Higher levels of the floodplain may be reached only during higher floods, such as a 100-year flood.

It is important to note that floodplains are an essential part of the river system that are extremely important in allowing the river to adjust to changing conditions. During floods the floodplains act to hold water, reducing the speed and height of floods in downstream areas, and the unconsolidated sediments in the floodplain also absorb large quantities of the water, reducing the amount that flows downstream. The floodplain also serves as a large temporary and mobile storage area for the sediments that have been eroded from throughout the watershed. This storage is important for maintaining the river's ability to respond to changes in discharge, climate, and other variables and therefore needs to remain in contact with the river. Attempts to isolate the floodplain from the river by construction of levees and artificial canals disrupt the natural flow and separate different components of the system, setting the stage for disasters.

STREAM TERRACES

Terraces are abandoned floodplains formed when a stream flowed above its present channel and floodplain level. These form when a stream erodes downward through its deposits to a new lower level. Paired terraces are terrace remnants that lie at the same elevation on either side of the present floodplain. Nonpaired terraces form at different levels on either side of the current floodplain and indicate several episodes of erosion. Rivers and streams may downcut through older terraces for a variety of reasons, including climatically influenced changes in discharge or uplift of the river valley and slopes, causing a change in the river profile.

DELTAS

When a stream enters the relatively still water of a lake or the ocean, its velocity and its capacity to hold sediment drop suddenly. Thus, the stream dumps its sediment load here, and the resulting deposit is known as a delta. Where a coarse sediment load of an alluvial fan dumps its load in a delta, the deposit is known as a fan delta. Braid deltas are formed when braided streams meet local base level and deposit their coarse-grained load. When a stream deposits its load in a delta, it first drops the coarsest material, then progressively finer material farther out, forming a distinctive sedimentary deposit. The resulting foreset layer is thus graded from coarse nearshore to fine offshore. The bottomset layer consists of the finest material, deposited far out. As this material continues to build outward, the stream must extend its length and forms new deposits, known as topset layers, on top of all this. Most of the world's large

False-color satellite images from the Moderate Resolution Imaging Spectroradiometer (image taken June 3, 2002) showing the Nile River and Delta. The Nile flows from south to north and carries sediment to the Nile Delta, the dark triangular-shaped area at the top of the image. Since many dams, including the Aswân High Dam, were built, the Nile carries less sediment, and the delta is beginning to erode. Also, the fertile Nile Valley is not flooded as often, so the fertilizing silts are no longer deposited on the floodplain. *(NASA)*

rivers have built huge deltas at their mouths such as the Mississippi, the Nile, and the Ganges, yet all of these are different in detail.

Drainage Systems

A *drainage basin* is the total area that contributes water to a stream, and the line that divides different drainage basins is known as a divide (such as the Continental Divide), or interfluve. Drainage basins are the primary landscape units or systems concerned with the collection and movement of water and sediment into streams and river channels. Drainage basins consist of a number of interrelated systems that work together to control the distribution and flow of water within the basin.

Hillslope processes, bedrock and surficial geology, vegetation, climate, and many other systems all interact in complex ways that determine where streams will form and how much water and sediment they will transport. A drainage basin's hydrologic dynamics can be analyzed by considering these systems along with how much water enters the basin through precipitation and how much leaves the basin in the discharge of the main trunk channel. Streams are arranged in an orderly fashion in drainage basins, with progressively smaller channels branching away from the main trunk channel. Stream channels are ordered and numbered according to this systematic branching. The smallest segments that lack tributaries are known as first-order streams; second-order streams form where two first-order streams converge. Third-order streams form where two second-order streams converge, and so on.

Streams within drainage basins develop characteristic branching patterns that reflect, to some degree, the underlying bedrock geology, structure, and rock types. *Dendritic drainage,* or randomly branching, patterns form on horizontal strata or on rocks with uniform erosional resistance. Parallel drainage patterns develop on steeply dipping strata or on areas with systems of parallel faults or other landforms. *Trellis drainage* patterns consist of parallel main stream channels intersected at nearly right angles by tributaries, in turn fed by tributaries parallel to the main channels. Trellis drainage patterns reflect significant structural

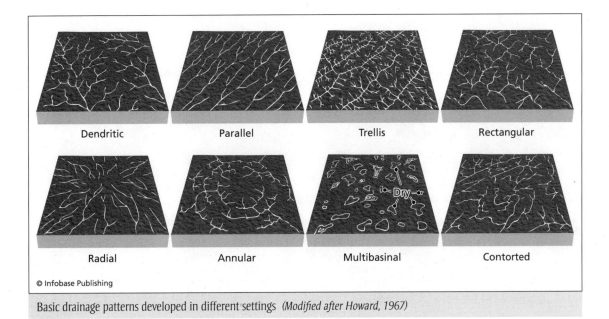

Basic drainage patterns developed in different settings *(Modified after Howard, 1967)*

control and typically form where eroded edges of alternating soft and hard layers are tilted, as in folded mountains or uplifted coastal strata. Rectangular drainage patterns form a regular rectangular grid on the surface and typically form in areas where the bedrock is strongly faulted or jointed. Radial and annular patterns develop on domes including volcanoes and other roughly circular uplifts. Other, more complex patterns are possible in more complex situations, as illustrated by multibasinal and contorted styles of drainage patterns.

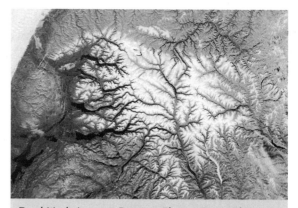

Dendritic drainage on Putorana Plateau, Russia. This image was taken September 25, 2003, by the Moderate Resolution Imaging Spectroradiometer aboard NASA's *Aqua* satellite. *(Jeff Schmaltz, MODIS Land Rapid Response Team at NASA, GSFC)*

Several categories of streams in drainage basins reflect different geologic histories. A *consequent stream* is one whose course is determined by the direction of the slope of the land. A *subsequent stream* is one whose course has become adjusted so that it occupies a belt of weak rock or another geologic structure. An *antecedent stream* is one that has maintained its course across topography that is being uplifted by tectonic forces; these cross high ridges. *Superposed streams* are those whose courses were laid down in overlying strata onto unlike strata below.

Aerial view of rivers cutting across rising mountains in the Macdonnell Ranges, Central Australia. The Kirchauff anticline has been truncated, and antecedent rivers form a trellis drainage pattern. *(© G. R. "Dick" Roberts/NSIL/Visuals Unlimited)*

Stream capture occurs when headland erosion diverts one stream and its drainage into another drainage basin.

Conclusion

Streams are very dynamic systems that represent a balance between the forces that drive the current and those that resist the flow. Channels have many different styles that form in response to a quasi-equilibrium between the gradient or slope of the streambed, the discharge of the stream, the amount of sediment being transported, the roughness of the streambed, and the resistance of the bank to erosion. The stream may form one of three main types of channels in response to the relative contributions of these variables. Straight channels are the most rare and are usually controlled by incision into a bedrock structure, but within the straight channel the current usually follows a curved path. Meandering streams are most common, with the current actively eroding cut banks and depositing material on the opposite point bars. In this way the meanders move back and forth across the floodplain, keeping an equilibrium through changes in the sinuosity, meander wavelength, width and depth of the channel, and velocity of the current. Meandering channels and their floodplains are different parts of the same dynamic system. Braided streams have multiple channels, are prone to rapid changes, and carry more sediment than meandering or straight channels. They are prone to large fluctuations in discharge and load, and many are found in environments in front of melting glaciers.

Individual stream and river channels are parts of much larger systems, and the patterns of branching and angles between individual streams often define different patterns that reflect underlying processes. Some river systems exhibit control by uniform slopes, some have rectilinear patterns reflecting underlying beds and structures, some are radial reflecting drainage off domes, and others cut straight through uplifted mountain ranges. The regional pattern of the stream channels reflects control by the underlying geology, and the more local stream channel pattern reflects control by the balance between the forces driving the current and those opposing the current. Streams can deposit thick layers of sand, mud, and gravel on floodplains; cut through them forming terraces; and carry massive amounts of sediment to the sea and deposit them as giant delta complexes. These delta complexes build to sea and have forms that reflect a balance between sediment input, tides, and wave energy. Many delta lobes are active on the order of 1,000 years, then the river switches course and forms a new lobe, as the older one subsides.

3

Effects of River Modifications and Urbanization on River Dynamics

The long history of flooding and attempted flood control measures along the Mississippi River Basin has taught engineers some valuable lessons on how to manage flood control on river basins. Levees are commonly built along riverbanks to protect towns and farmlands from river floods. These levees are usually successful at the job they were intended to do, but they also cause some other collateral effects. First, the levees do not allow waters to spill onto the floodplains, so the floodplains do not receive the annual fertilization by thin layers of silt, and they may begin to deflate and slowly degrade as a result of this loss of nourishment by the river. The ancient Egyptians relied on such yearly floods to maintain their fields' productivity, which has declined since the Nile has been dammed and altered in recent times. Another effect of levees is that they constrict the river to a narrow channel so that floodwaters that once spread slowly over a large region are now focused into a narrow space. This causes floods to rise faster, reach greater heights, have a greater velocity, and reach downstream areas faster than rivers without levees. The extra speed of the river is in many cases enough to erode the levees and return the river to its natural state.

One of the less appreciated effects of building levees on the sides of rivers is that they sometimes cause the river to slowly rise above the height of the floodplain. Many rivers naturally aggrade, or accumulate

Unbroken levee along the Mississippi River *(E. R. Degginger/Photo Researchers, Inc.)*

sediment along their bottoms. In a natural system without levees this aggradation is accompanied by lateral or sideways migration of the channel so that the river stays at the same height with time. However, if a levee is constructed and maintained, the river is forced to stay in the same location as it builds up its bottom. As the bottom rises, the river naturally adds to the height of the levee, and people will also build up the height of the levee as the river rises to prevent further flooding. The net result is that the river may gradually rise above the floodplain until some catastrophic flood causes the levee to break, and the river establishes a new course.

The process of breaking through a levee happens naturally as well and is known as avulsion. Avulsion has occurred seven times in the last 6,000 years along the lower Mississippi River. Each time the river has broken through a levee a few hundred miles from the mouth of the river and has found a new shorter route to the Gulf of Mexico. The old river channel and delta is then abandoned, and the delta subsides below sea level, as the river no longer replenishes it. A new channel is established, and this gradually builds up a new delta until it too is abandoned in favor of a younger shorter channel to the gulf.

In this chapter the history of constructing levees along the Mississippi River is examined, as it illustrates how the dynamics of the river were not appreciated as the course of the river was being altered and how levees constructed to reduce flooding and increase navigability were constricting the flow. By the time engineers realized the consequences of constricting the river, a couple of hundred years of river modifications had already taken their toll. Still, further modifications were proposed and implemented, and the floods continue to get worse. The history of levee construction, destruction by floods, and the subsequent reconstruction are discussed in this chapter and in chapter 4, where more human aspects of some of the historical floods are presented. The second section of this chapter deals with urbanization of the floodplain and how this has also dramatically altered the river-floodplain dynamics and ecosystems and increased the flood risks for people along many river valleys of the world.

History of Levee Building on the Mississippi River

The Mississippi River drainage basin is the largest in the United States and encompasses the third-largest watershed in the world, draining 41 percent of the continental United States, including an area of 1,245,000 square miles (3,224,550 km²). The river transports 230 million tons of sediment, including the sixth largest silt load in the world. Before the Europeans came and began altering the river, this fertile silt used to cover the floodplains during the semi-annual floods and then be carried downriver and deposited in the Mississippi River Delta. Levee construction along the lower Mississippi River began with the first settlers who came to the region and has continued until the present-day levee system, the main parts of which include 2,203 miles (3,580 km) of levees, floodwalls, and other control structures. Of this, 1,607 miles (2,586 km) of levees lie along the Mississippi River, and another 596 miles (959 km) are along the banks of the Arkansas and Red Rivers in the Atchafalaya Basin. Additional levees have been built along the Missouri River.

The first levee along the Mississippi was built around the first iteration of New Orleans between 1718 and 1727 and consisted of slightly more than a mile-long (5,400 feet, or 1,646 m), four-foot- (1.2-m-) high earthen mound that was 18 feet (5.5 m) wide at the top, with a road along the crown. This levee was meant to protect the residents of the newly founded city from annual floods and pestilence that would occur from March until June of each year. New Orleans had only recently been inhabited; Louis XIV had commissioned the explorer Pierre Le Moyne,

(opposite) Map of the lower Mississippi River, from the mouth of the delta to southern Missouri, showing the thousands of miles of levees that have been constructed along the river in the past century

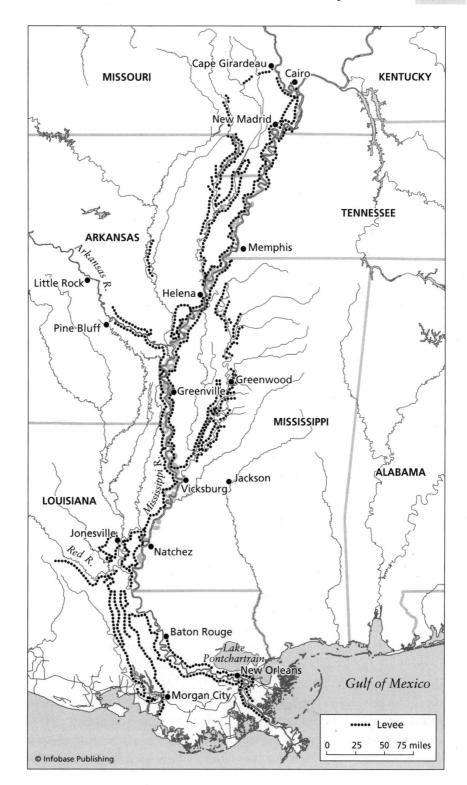

sieur d'Iberville, to establish a colony near the mouth of the Mississippi River to control the Mississippi Valley and the lumber and fur trade moving down the river. Iberville's younger brother, Jean-Baptiste Le Moyne, sieur de Bienville, established New Orleans in 1718 in a bend of the river to control the portage between the Mississippi River and Lake Pontchartrain. The site of New Orleans was surrounded by water on all sides. Lakes Ponchartrain, Maurepas, and Bayou Manchac and the Amite River divide it from higher land on the north, and the Mississippi River wraps around its other sides. The site of New Orleans on the natural levee of the Mississippi on the Isle of Orleans has always been precarious, and the city has been inundated by floods from the river on three sides, as well as by *storm surges* from *hurricanes* on the other side about every 30 years since its founding. The first levee built in 1718–27 did not stop the floods, and on September 23–24, 1722, a large hurricane nearly completely destroyed the newly founded capital city. The storm had 100 mile per hour (161 kph) sustained winds and a storm surge of seven to eight feet (2–2.4 m) that overtopped the four-foot-high levee. Almost every building in the city was destroyed or severely damaged. If city planners had taken this warning when the city only consisted of several dozens of buildings, much damage could have been avoided in the future; instead, more and higher levees were built, with successive floods by storms destroying or severely damaging the city in 1812, 1819, 1837, 1856, 1893, 1909, 1915, 1947, 1956, 1965, 1969, and 2004. Just as the old levees did not hold in 1722, the new levees did not hold in 2004 during Hurricanes Katrina and Rita, and the levees broke repeatedly during the high-water events in between.

The early river levees along the Mississippi consisted of earthen mounds, generally with a slope of 1:2. The local and state governments made it a policy that local farmers had to build their own levees along the property they owned along the Mississippi River. Haul methods for bringing the dirt to make the levees were primitive, typically with horse and carriage, yielding only 10–12 cubic yards (7.5–9 m³) per day. The federal government became involved in 1820 with legislation that was focused mostly on navigation along the river and did not consider flood control. As the levees were built at break-neck pace, the river became constricted, and this caused the bed of the river to continuously raise itself in a process called aggradation. This happens because if the river is not allowed to migrate laterally, it cannot move the sediment it is carrying and depositing out of the way and cannot widen the channel, so it therefore raises the bed as this sediment is deposited. Disastrous floods along the lower Mississippi River in 1844, 1849, and 1850 resulted in passage of the Swamp Acts of 1849 and 1850. These acts gave the states of Louisiana, Mississippi, Arkansas, Missouri, and Illinois swamp and overflow lands within these states boundaries that were unfit for cultivation. These lands were sold, and the revenues generated were used to construct levees and complete drainage reclamation of the purchased lands. Between 1850 and 1927 the levees along the lower Mississippi had to be continuously heightened, because of this river avulsion caused by the construction of the levees.

In 1850 U.S. Congress appropriated $50,000 to complete two topographic and hydrographic surveys in an effort to promote flood protection along the Mississippi River. One survey was completed by a civilian engineer, Charles Ellet, Jr., and the other by army engineers A. A. Humphreys and Henry Abbot. The Humphreys-Abbot report recommended three possible methods for flood control: cutting off the bends in the river; diversion of tributaries, creating artificial reservoirs and outlets; and confining the river to its channel using levees. Since the first two options were considered too expensive, the third was enacted, with long-lasting consequences. Their levee design called for levees to be built to a height of 3–11 feet (0.9–3.4 m) above the level of the 1858 flood.

During the Civil War, from 1861 to 1865, the levees fell into a state of disrepair, made worse by the large floods of 1862, 1865, and 1867. Floods in 1874 prompted the creation of a Levee Commission to complete a new survey of the state of the levees and make recommendations for how to repair the system and reclaim the floodplain. The Levee Commission made a stark assessment, citing major defects in the system and huge costs to repair and improve the system. They documented that previous levees had been built in faulty locations, with poor organization and construction, insufficient height, and inadequate inspection and guarding. They estimated that it would cost $3.5 million to repair the existing system, and $46 million to build a new, complete levee system to reclaim the floodplain from the river.

In 1879 the Mississippi River Commission (MRC) was created by Congress, as organized by James B. Eads. The commission consisted of three officers from the U.S. Army Corps of Engineers, three civilians, and one officer from the U.S. Coast and Geodetic Survey. The MRC conducted surveys and suggested many modifications and new additions to the flood control and navigation projects along the river. The commission made a policy in 1882 to close the breaks along the levee and to construct a line of levees with sufficient height and grade to supposedly contain the frequent floods along the river. The faults in the MRC model were soon evident.

The flood of 1890 destroyed 56 miles (90 km) of levees, and the MRC began to raise the levees from 38 to 46 feet (11.5–14 m). During this phase of massive reconstruction the federal government and private citizens added more than 125 million cubic yards (96 million m³) of soil to the levees, but much of this was lost to the river by mass wasting processes including slumping and bank caving. Efforts were made to reenforce the banks with various structures to make them stronger, but then the flood of 1912 came, again destroying much of the levee system that was meant to protect the adjacent floodplain. The response of the commission was to raise the levees again, to three feet above the 1912 flood line. The lesson that raising the levee and constricting the river causes the bed to aggrade and rise as well was not yet learned.

The first federal flood control act was passed in 1917, authorizing levees to be built for flood control both along the Mississippi and its tributaries. The federal government would pay two-thirds of the costs of levees if the local interests would pay the other third. During the 1920s levee construction was stepped up to a quicker pace with the mechanization of earth-moving technology and the introduction of large cranes, moving tower machines, and cableway draglines.

In 1927 came the greatest flood in recorded history along the lower Mississippi River Valley. Many of the levees built to the MRC standards failed up and down the river, with enormous consequences in terms of loss of life, displaced people, and loss of property that was supposed to be protected by the levees. The government responded with the 1928 Flood Control Act, bringing legislation to improve the grade of the levees and make models of different flood scenarios, including the creation of several large floodways that could be opened to let water out of the river in high-flow times. Some of these floodways were quite large, such as the Birds Point–New Madrid Floodway, which is about 35 miles (56 km) long and 3–10 miles (5–16 km) wide, designed to divert 550,000 cubic feet (15,576 m³) per second of flow from the Mississippi during floods. Further downriver the West Atchafalaya Floodway was designed to be able to carry half of the modeled project flood of 1,500,000 cubic feet (139,400 m³) per second. The Bonnet Carre Floodway was built upriver from New Orleans, designed to restrict the flow to downstream by diverting the water and thereby protecting New Orleans. Levees were redesigned and moved to locations where their projected lifespan was from 20 to 30 years and thought to be more resistant. As the construction on the new levee and floodway system continued, new floods, such as in 1929, disrupted operations, but the construction methods continued to improve. Many of the levees built form part of the present-day levee system.

In 1937 a large flood emanated from the Ohio River watershed, raising the waters to levels such that the Birds Point–New Madrid Floodway was opened by dynamiting the Fuse Plus levee. This released huge volumes of water and eased the flood downstream. One of the lessons from the 1937 flood was that roads should be added to the levees, to aid in moving material from place to place during floods. In 1947 the MRC began redesigning levees to be stronger to avoid failure, recognizing the importance of *compaction* for reducing the chances of levee failure.

Levees fail by three main modes; underseepage of water beneath the levee, where the pressure from the high water opens a channel causing catastrophic failure; *hydraulic piping*, in which the water finds a weak passage through the levee; and overtopping, when the water flows over the top of the levee and erodes the sides. Levees can also fail when the river current scours the base of the levee during high-flow conditions,

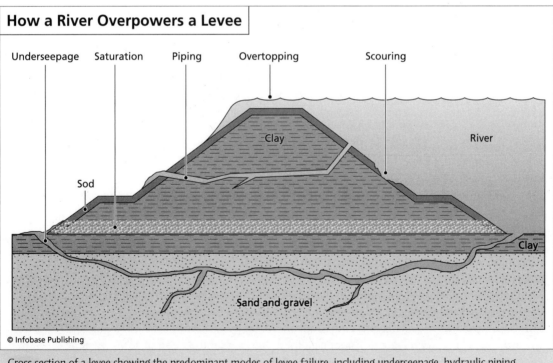

Cross section of a levee showing the predominant modes of levee failure, including underseepage, hydraulic piping, scouring, and overtopping *(Modified from U.S. Army Corps of Engineers)*

as happened in many of the Mississippi River floods, and this causes slumping and massive collapse of the levee. Mass wasting is also promoted by long-term floods in which the water gradually saturates the pores of the levee, weakening it, causing massive liquefaction and catastrophic failure, and leading large sections of the levee to collapse at the same time. Most levee failures happen during time periods when the flow has been high for long periods, as this increases the *pore pressure,* scouring, and liquefaction potential of the levee.

CHARLES BANKS BELT, JR.: PIONEER IN UNDERSTANDING FLOOD HAZARDS FROM LEVEE CONSTRUCTION

Charles B. Belt, Jr., was born in New York City on December 12, 1931, first child of Charles Banks Belt, who was in real estate management in New York City, and his wife, Emma Willard Scudder Keyes Belt, a descendant of Emma Willard, who had founded the first school for girls in the East in 1816. The Belts moved to the eastern end of Long Island. Belt's father was an amateur naturalist and member of the Explorers Club. In college Belt majored in geology at Williams College, in Williamstown Massachusetts, and received a B.S. in 1953. He received an MA in 1955 and a Ph.D. in 1958 from Columbia University, New York City. Belt spent a year from April 1958 to April 1959 working as a geologist in Belo Horizonte, Brazil, for the M. A. Hanna Co. on a large iron ore deposit at Pico da Itabira, a few months in 1959 as a sampler in Butte, Montana, for the Anaconda Copper Co., and a year or so in Murray, Utah, working for the exploration arm of Kennecott Copper Co.

He came to St. Louis University (SLU) in 1961 to teach geology in the Department of Earth and Atmospheric Sciences. He taught the first course offered in environmental geology at SLU in the early 1970s. In 1973 the Mississippi River overflowed its banks in St. Louis. The Coalition for the Environment had recently been founded, with Belt and his wife, Louise McKeon Belt, among the founding members. The commission's president, Lewis C. Green, arranged for hydrologist Luna Leopold to speak at the annual dinner that year. Green and Belt drove Leopold around to see the flood effects. In his speech that weekend on the flood, Leopold emphasized the need to research and quantify whether there were effects the Corps of Engineers projects had had on flood levels on the big rivers. Belt took on the task. He bought a handheld calculator and got to work evenings and weekends, spending his own spare time on the project. The result was a peer reviewed paper published in *Science* in 1975. This paper was one of the first to present quantitative data that showed that the construction of levees, wing dikes, and other navigational works caused the river flood stages to be higher than without the changes to the river, for the same amount of water flowing in the rivers. Charlie Belt's work was instrumental to the current understanding of the hazards of constricting rivers through the construction of levees, the harm that levees cause the natural ecosystems of floodplains, and the hazards levees pose to those whose livelihoods depend on floodplains. After publication of the 1975 paper, Charlie Belt spent the next 20 years researching floods and was working on the flood of 1993 when he died after being hit by a car. The methods of flood stage analyses devised by Charlie Belt are now used around the world in river planning.

Loading sandbags onto an area where the levee has broken, New Orleans, September 9, 2005 *(FEMA)*

By 1956 the MRC was modeling floods with twice the discharge as it previously had, examining the ability of the river and levee system to handle a discharge of 3,000,000 cubic feet (2,300,000 m³) per second. The flood of 1973 hit the Mississippi River Basin with one of the highest floods recorded in 200 years. The flood also set a record for the number of days the river was out of bank, causing more than $183,756,000 in damages. In terms of flood management the flood of 1973 brought about the realization that building levees, wing dikes, and other navigational and so-called flood control measures had actually decreased the carrying capacity of the river, meaning that for any given amount of water, the flood levels (called stages) would be higher than before the levees were built. This was documented in a landmark paper in *Science* by Charles B. Belt, Jr., entitled "The 1973 Flood and Man's Constriction of the Mississippi River" (see sidebar on page 46).

The catastrophic floods of 1993 provided another test of the levees, and the new system failed massively. The constriction of the river caused by the levees led to numerous cases of levee failure, overtopping, crevasse splays, collapse, and massive amounts of damage as had never been seen before along the river. Approximately two-thirds of all the levees in the upper Mississippi River Basin collapsed, were breached, or were otherwise damaged by the floods of 1993. Dozens of people died, and 50,000 homes were damaged or destroyed, with a total damage estimate exceeding a billion dollars.

Urbanization and Flash Flooding

Urbanization is the process of building up and populating a natural habitat or environment such that the habitat or environment no longer responds to input the way it did before being altered by humans. When heavy rains fall in an unaltered natural environment, the land surface responds to accommodate the additional water. Desert regions may experience severe erosion in response to the force of falling raindrops that dislodge soil and also by overland flow during heavy rains. This causes upland channel areas to enlarge, becoming able to accommodate larger floods. Areas that frequently receive heavy rains may develop lush vegetative cover, which helps to break the force of the raindrops and reduce soil erosion, and the extensive root system holds the soil in place against erosion by overland flow. Stream channels may be large so that they can accommodate large-volume floods.

When the natural system is altered in urban areas, the result can be dangerous. Many municipalities have paved over large parts of drainage basins and covered much of the *recharge area* with roads, buildings, parking lots, and other structures. The result is that much of the water that used to seep into the ground and infiltrate into the groundwater system now flows overland into stream channels, which may themselves be modified or even paved over. The net effect of these alterations is that flash floods may occur much more frequently than in a natural system since more water flows into the stream system than before the alterations. The floods may occur with significantly lower amounts of rainfall as well, and as the water flows overland without slowly seeping into the ground, the flash floods may reach urban areas more quickly than the floods did before the alterations to the stream system. Overall, the effect of urbanization is faster, stronger, bigger floods, which have greater erosive power and do more damage. It is almost as if the natural environment responds to urban growth by increasing its ability to return the environment to its natural state.

Urbanization and Changes to the Missouri River Floodplain

The Missouri River stretches more than 2,300 miles (3,700 km) and drains one-sixth of the United States. It was once one of the wildest stretches of rivers in the American Midwest. During the past two centuries the Missouri River and its adjacent wetlands and floodplains have been dramatically modified in various attempts to promote transportation, agriculture, and development. These modifications have included draining wetlands for cultivation, straightening stream channels to facilitate navigation, stabilizing banks to prevent erosion, and constructing agricultural levees, dams, reservoirs, and flood control levees to control water flow and exclude floodwaters from the floodplain. These modifications have resulted in a severe loss of wetlands.

Wing dikes on the Missouri River, looking east at Jefferson City, Missouri, circa 1960. The wing dikes change the flow of the river and cause the river to deposit sand and mud, thereby making the channel become narrower. *(Missouri State Archives)*

Historically, the Missouri River floodplain below Sioux City, Iowa, covered 1.9 million acres (7,689 km²). According to the Sierra Club (in legal case 03-04254-CV-C-SOW of *Sierra Club v. US Army Corps of Engineers*) modifications to the river-floodplain system described above have resulted in the loss of approximately 168,000 acres of natural channel, 354,000 acres (1,433 km²) of meander belt habitat, and 50 percent of the Missouri River's surface. In addition, shallow-water habitat has been reduced by up to 90 percent in some areas while sandbars, islands, oxbows, and backwaters have been virtually eliminated. Forested floodplains along the Missouri River have decreased from 76 percent in the 19th century to 13 percent in 1972, and cultivated lands have increased from 18 percent to 83 percent.

By the late 1970s the lower Missouri River had been totally channelized, and its natural floodplain ecosystems, almost completely converted to agricultural or other uses. Today the lower Missouri River is flanked by levees and other flood control structures for most of its length. Environmental groups, such as the Sierra Club, Great Rivers Habitat Alliance, and Ducks Unlimited, have been fighting further development of the floodplain in an effort to prevent the complete loss of this habitat and to reduce the risks of hazardous floods along the system.

The Los Angeles River, photographed on April 21, 2006, is completely paved over, so the river channel has no chance to follow its natural pattern. *(Getty)*

Modifications and Channelization of Rivers for Use by Growing Populations

Some desert and semi-arid regions of the world have undergone rapid population explosions, necessitating the alteration of river courses to bring water to thirsty cities and to provide irrigation to farmlands to feed this growing population. In the U.S. Southwest, in California, in China, and in the Middle East, riverways have been extensively modified, regulated, and even diverted hundreds of miles from their natural courses to provide water to places where people prefer to live.

Many examples of the effects of urbanization on flood intensity have been documented from California and the Southwest. Urban areas such as Los Angeles, San Diego, Tucson, Phoenix, and other cities have documented the speed and severity of floods from similar rainfall amounts along the same drainage basin. What these studies have documented is that the floodwaters rise much more quickly after urbanization, and they rise up to four times the height of pre-urbanization, depending on the extent of pavement over the surface. The increased speed at which the floodwaters rise and the increased height to which they rise are directly correlated with the amount of land surface that is now covered over by roads, houses, and parking lots, blocking infiltration.

In natural systems floods gradually wane after the highest peak passes, and the slow fall of the floodwaters is related to the stream system being recharged by groundwater that has seeped into the shallow

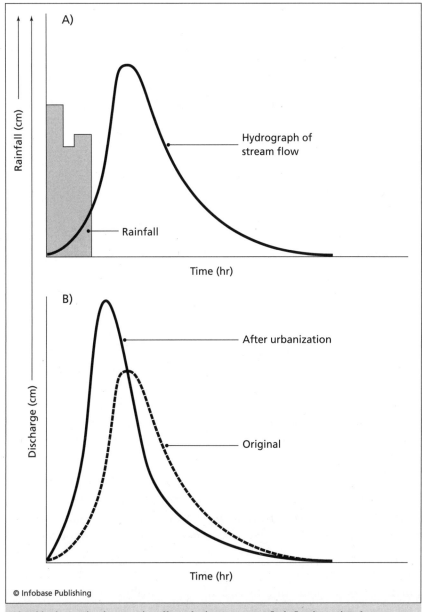

Flood hydrographs showing the effect of urbanization on flash flooding. A) Before urbanization rivers rise slowly after a rainfall and also recede slowly. B) After urbanization the flood rises much faster, reaches greater heights, and disappears faster than in non-urbanized areas. *(Modified from USGS)*

surface area during the heavy rainfall event. However, in urbanized areas the floodwaters not only rise quickly but also recede faster than in the natural environment. This is attributed to the lack of groundwater continuing to recharge the stream after the flood peak in urbanized areas.

Many other modifications to stream channels have been made in urbanized areas, with limited success in changing nature's course to suit human needs. Many stream channels have been straightened, which only causes the water to flow faster and have more erosive power. Straightening the stream course also shortens the stream length and thereby steepens the gradient. The stream may respond to this by aggrading and filling the channel with sediment, in an attempt to regain the natural gradient.

UNITED STATES SOUTHWESTERN DESERT

The history of development of the American Southwest was crucially dependent on bringing water resources into this semi-arid region. Much of California, especially the Los Angeles region, was regarded as worthless desert scrubland until huge water projects designed by the Bureau of Land Reclamation diverted rivers and resources from all over the West. In the years between 1911 and 1923 the California water department, under the leadership of William Mulholland, quietly purchased most of the water rights to the Owens Valley at the foot of the Sierra Nevada and then constructed a 233-mile- (373-km-) long aqueduct to bring this water to Los Angeles. When the local Owens Valley ranchers saw their water supplies dry up, they repeatedly dynamited the aqueduct until Mulholland effectively declared war on the ranchers of Owens Valley, protecting the aqueduct with a massive show of armed force. This was the beginning of the present-day California aqueduct system, forming the branch known as the Los Angeles Aqueduct.

The California aqueduct is presently 444 miles (715 km) long, and much of it consists of a concrete-lined channel that is typically 40 feet (12 m) wide and 30 feet (9 m) deep. The aqueduct has several sections, one starting at the San Joaquin-Sacramento River delta, to the San Luis Reservoir, then south to Los Angeles with a branch in between heading to the coast. The California aqueduct meets the Los Angeles Aqueduct north of Los Angeles, and the two systems distribute their water to the valley and thirsty residents of the city.

In the late 1800s geologist and explorer John Wesley Powell explored the West and warned that the water resources in the region were not

Map of California showing the locations of the aqueducts bringing water from the mountains of the Sierra Nevada and from Mono Lake to water-thirsty Los Angeles

sufficient for extensive settlement of the Southwest. However, Congress went forward with a series of massive dam projects along the Colorado River, including the Hoover Dam, Glen Canyon Dam, and countless others across the region. These dams changed natural canyons and wild rivers into passive reservoirs that now feed large cities, including Phoenix, Tuscon, Las Vegas, Los Angeles, and San Diego. Use of water from the Colorado became so extensive that by 1969, whereas the river once flowed to the sea, no more water was flowing in the lower Colorado, the

The California aqueduct in Central Valley, California. The Sierra Nevada is in the background. *(Harris Schiffman, 2007, used under license from Shutterstock, Inc.)*

delta environment had been destroyed, and water that Mexico used to rely on was no longer available.

Reliance on distant water sources to live in a desert may not seem the wisest of decisions, but much of the population of California and the southwestern desert is living off of water diverted from resources in the Owens Valley, the Trinity River, the Colorado River, and many other western sources. Some conservationists, such as M. Reisner (author of *Cadillac Desert*, 1986), paint a picture of development of the U.S. Southwest that is ominous and has many parallels to ill-fated societies elsewhere in the history of the world. It is becoming increasingly difficult to continue to expand development in the desert and demand more and more water resources from a depleting source. Many of the soils are becoming too salty to sustain agriculture. With predictions of global climate change and expanding deserts, the future of the region needs to be critically examined so the nation can prepare for further, deeper water crises.

WATER, POLITICS, AND THE MIDDLE EAST

Water shortage or drought coupled with rapid population growth provide for extreme volatility for any region. In the Middle East water shortage issues go hand in hand with longstanding political and religious differences. The Middle East region, stretching from North Africa and the Arabian Peninsula, up through Israel and Lebanon to Turkey, and over to the Tigris-Euphrates Valley, has only three major river systems and a few smaller rivers. Its population stands at about 160 million people. The Nile has an annual discharge of about 82 billion cubic yards (62.7 billion m³), whereas the combined Tigris-Euphrates system has an annual discharge of 93 billion cubic yards (71 billion m³). Some of the most serious water-politics and drought issues in the Middle East arise from the four states that share the relatively small amounts of water of the Jordan River, with an annual discharge of less than 2 billion cubic yards (1.5 billion m³). It has been estimated that with current water usage and population growth, many nations in this region have only 10–15 years left before the agriculture and eventual security of these nations will be seriously threatened.

The region is arid, receiving 1–8 inches (2.5–20 cm) of rain per year and has many drought years with virtually no rain. The Middle East has a population growth rate of about 3.5 percent per year—one of the fastest in the world—and many countries in the region have inefficient agricultural practices that contribute to the growing problem of desertification in the region. Some of the problems include planting of water-intensive crops, common flooding and furrow methods of irrigation, as well as spraying types of irrigation that lose much of the water to evaporation, and poor management of water and crop resources. These growing demands on the limited water supply, coupled with political strife resulting from shared usage of waterways that flow through multiple countries, has set the region up for a major confrontation over water rights. Many of the region's past and present leaders have warned that water issues may be the cause of the next major conflict in the Middle East. In the words of the late king Hussein of Jordan, water issues "could drive nations of the region to war."

Water use by individuals is by necessity much less in countries in the Middle East than in the United States and in other Western countries. For instance, in the United States every American has about 11,000 cubic yards (8,410 m³) of freshwater potential to use each year, while citizens of Iraq (using prewar figures) have about 6,000 cubic yards (4,590 m³); of Turkey, 4,400 cubic yards (3,364 m³); and of Syria, about 3,000 cubic yards (2,294 m³). Along the Nile, Egyptians have about 1,200 cubic yards (917 m³) available per year for each citizen.

In the Levant, Israelis have a freshwater potential of 500 cubic yards (382 m³) per person per year, and Jordanians have only 280 cubic yards (214 m³) per year.

The Nile, the second longest river on Earth, forms the main water supply for nine North African nations, and disputes have grown over how to share this water with growing demands. The Blue Nile flows out of the Ethiopian Highlands and meets the White Nile in Sudan north of Khartoum then flows through northern Sudan and into Egypt. The Nile is dammed at Aswān, forming Lake Nasser, then flows north through the fertile valley of Egypt to the Mediterranean.

The Nile is the only major river in Egypt, and nearly all of Egypt's population lives in the Nile Valley. About 3 percent of the nation's arable land stretches along the Nile Valley, but 80 percent of Egypt's water use goes to agriculture in the valley. The government has been attempting to improve agricultural and irrigation techniques, which in many places have not changed considerably for 5,000 years. If the Egyptians embraced widespread use of drip irrigation and other modern agricultural practices, the demands on water could easily be reduced by 50 percent, or more.

Egypt has initiated a massive construction and national reconstruction project with the aim of establishing a second branch of the Nile River, extending from Lake Nasser in the south across the scorching Western Desert and emerging at the sea at Alexandria. This ambitious project starts in the Tushka Canal area, where water is drained from Lake Nasser and steered into a topographic depression that winds its way north through some of the hottest, driest desert landscape on Earth. The government has been moving thousands of farmers and industrialists from the familiar Nile Valley into this national frontier, hoping to alleviate overcrowding. Cairo's population of 15 million is increasing at a rate of nearly 1 million per year. If successful, this plan could reduce the water demands on the limited resources of the river.

There are many obstacles to this plan. Will people stay in a desert where temperatures regularly exceed 120°F (49°C)? Will the water make it to Alexandria, having to flow through unsaturated sands and through a region where the evaporation rate is 200 times greater than the precipitation rate? How will drifting sands and blowing dust affect plans for agriculture in the Western Desert? Much of the downriver part of

(opposite) Map of the Middle East showing the main river systems. The area faces the complications of a rapidly growing population and a severe lack of water.

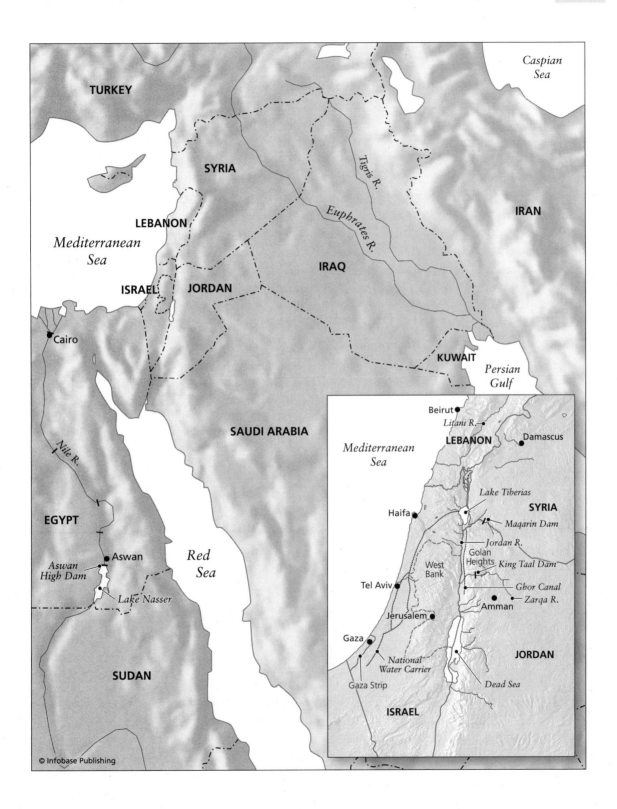

the Nile is suffering from lower water and silt levels than needed to sustain agriculture or even the current land surface. So much water is used, diverted, or dammed upstream that parts of the Nile Delta have actually started to subside (sink) beneath sea level. These regions desperately need to receive the annual silt layer from the flooding Nile to rebuild the land surface and keep it from disappearing beneath the sea.

There are also political problems with establishing the new river through the Western Desert. Ethiopia contributes about 85 percent of the water to the Nile, yet it is experiencing severe drought and famine in the eastern part of the country. There is no infrastructure to get the water from the Nile to the thirsty lands and people to the east. Sudan and Egypt have longstanding disputes over water allotments, and Sudan is not happy that Egypt is establishing a new river that will further Egyptian use of the water. Water is currently flowing out of Lake Nasser, filling up several small lake depressions to the west, and sinking into and evaporating between the sands.

The Jordan River Basin is host to some of the most severe drought and water shortage issues in the Middle East. Israel, Jordan, Syria, Lebanon, and the Palestinians share the Jordan River water, and the resource is much more limited than water along the Nile or in the Tigris-Euphrates system. The Jordan River is short (100 miles; 160 km) and consists of three main tributaries, each with different characteristics. The Hasbani River has a source in the mountains of Lebanon and flows south to Lake Tiberias, and the Banias flows from Syria into the lake. The smaller Dan River flows from Israel. The Jordan River then flows out of Lake Tiberias and is joined by water from the Yarmuk flowing out of Syria into the Dead Sea, where any unused water evaporates.

The Jordan River is the source for about 60 percent of the water used in Israel, and 75 percent of the water used in Jordan. The other water used by these countries is largely from groundwater aquifers. Israel has almost exclusive use of the coastal aquifer along the Mediterranean shore, whereas disputes arise over use of aquifers from the West Bank and Golan Heights. These areas are mountainous, get more rain and snowfall than the other parts of the region, and have some of the richest groundwater deposits in the region. Since the 1967 war Israel has tapped the groundwater beneath the West Bank and now gets approximately 30–50 percent of its water supply from groundwater reserves beneath the mountains of the West Bank. The Palestinians get about 80 percent of their water from this mountain aquifer. A similar situation exists for the Golan Heights, though with lower amounts of reserves. These areas therefore have attained a new significance in terms of regional negotiations for peace in the region.

The main problems of water use stem from the shortage of water compared to the population, effectively making drought conditions. The situation is not likely to improve given the alarming 3.5 percent annual population growth rate. Conservation efforts have only marginally improved the water use problem, and it is unlikely that there will be widespread rapid adoption throughout the region of many of the drip-irrigation techniques already used in Israel. This is partly because it takes a larger initial investment in drip irrigation than in conventional furrow and flooding types of irrigation systems. Many of the farmers cannot afford this investment, even if it would improve their long-term yields and decrease their use of water. In fact, when the Gaza Strip was turned over to Palestinian control, local Palestinian mobs ripped out the drip-irrigation systems and greenhouses set up by the Israelis and sold the parts for scrap. As a result more water is now needed to yield the same crops.

Sporadic droughts have made this situation worse in recent years, such that in 1999 Israel cut in half the amount of water it supplies to Jordan, and Jordan declared drought conditions and mandated water rationing. Jordan currently uses 73 percent of its water for irrigation, and if this number could be reduced by adoption of more efficient drip irrigation, the current situation would be largely under control.

One possible way to alleviate the problem of the drought and water shortage would be to explore for water in unconventional aquifer systems, such as fractures or faults, which are plentiful in the region. Many faults are porous and permeable structures that are several tens of feet wide and thousands of feet long and deep. They may be thought of as vertical aquifers, holding as much water as conventional aquifers. If these countries were to successfully explore for and exploit water in these structures, the water shortage and regional tensions might be reduced. This technique has proven effective in many other places in the Middle East, Africa, and elsewhere and would probably work here as well.

Another set of problems plague the Tigris-Euphrates drainage basin and the countries that share water along their course. There are many political differences between the countries of Turkey, Syria, and Iraq, and the Kurdish people have been fighting for an independent homeland in this region for more than a decade. One of the underlying causes of dispute in this region is also the scarce water supply in a drought-plagued area. Turkey is completing a massive dam construction campaign, with the largest dam being the Ataturk on the Euphrates. Overall, Turkey is spending an estimated $32 billion on 22 dams and 19 hydroelectric plants. The aim is to increase the irrigated land in Turkey by 40 percent and to supply 25 percent of the nation's electricity through the hydroelectric plants. This system of dams also now allows Turkey to control the flow of the Tigris and the Euphrates, and if it pleases, Turkey can virtually shut off the water supply to its downstream neighbors. At present Turkey is supplying Syria and Iraq with what it considers to be a reasonable amount of water, but what Syria and Iraq claim is inadequate. Political strife and even military action have resulted. Turkey is currently building a pipeline to bring water to drought-stricken Cyprus. Turkey and Israel are forging new partnerships and have been exploring ways to export water from Turkey and import it to Israel, which could help the drought in the Levant.

Conclusion

People have modified rivers and floodplains for navigation and flood control for thousands of years, often with disastrous results. In the United States construction of levees along the Mississippi River began essentially as soon as European settlers arrived in the New Orleans area. Time and again levees were built, floods seemed to become larger, and the levees were breached or collapsed through processes of under-seepage, piping, scouring, or liquefaction. Some scientists noticed that as the levees were built higher, the base of the river seemed to aggrade, or rise, as well. However, it took 250 years before quantitative evidence was presented that the construction of levees and other flood control measures constricted the river and caused flood stages to rise higher and faster and become more dangerous, with increasing constriction of the river by levees. This understanding has not reached policy level in the United States, as rivers are still being actively constricted by levees, and floodplains are being widely developed.

Urbanization of floodplains also causes floods to rise faster, be more powerful, and do more damage than in natural settings. Some places in the world, such as the U.S. Southwest and parts of the Middle East, have extensively altered the natural drainage network to provide drinking and irrigation water for people in arid and semi-arid climates. These water resources are presently extremely stressed and are reaching their limits, yet the population keeps on expanding at alarming rates. New sources of water must be sought to meet the demands of a growing global population.

4

Examples of Flood Disasters

Floods are the most common natural hazard and also have proven to be the deadliest and costliest of all natural disasters in history. Individual floods have killed upward of a million people in China on several occasions and cause billions of dollars of damage annually in different parts of the world. The risk of flooding is becoming greater with time, as many countries are allowing people to move onto floodplains and even encouraging commercial and residential growth on floodplains that are known to experience floods at frequencies of every several to every couple of hundred years. As the population of the world continues to grow and people move into harm's way on floodplains, this problem will only get worse. Further, as the climate changes, some areas will experience more rainfall, while others will experience drought, so areas that may be relatively safe on floodplains now, may be frequently inundated with floodwaters in the near future. Development of floodplains should not proceed without proper scientific analysis of the risks. In most cases floodplains should be preserved as natural areas or used for farming but should not be the sites of major commercial or residential development.

There are several kinds of floods that affect different areas, act on different time scales, and have different types of hazards. There are floods associated with hurricanes and tidal surges in coastal areas, which can do extreme damage during these coastal storms. A second type of flood is known as a flash flood and is typically caused by rare large thunderstorms in mountains and canyon territory. These floods

A boy chops large ice chunks to clear a path to his house in Fort Fairfield, Maine, in April 1994. An ice jam on the Aroostook River caused a flood that did $6 million in damages. (AP)

can move into areas as a mud- and debris-laden wall of water, wiping out buildings and towns in a few seconds to minutes. A third category of floods are called regional floods, caused by prolonged rains over large drainage basins. A final type of flood occurs in areas where rivers freeze over. In cold climate zones the annual spring breakup can cause severe floods, initiated when blocks of ice get jammed behind islands, bridges, or along bends in rivers. These ice dams can create severe floods, causing the high spring waters to rise quickly and bring the ice-cold waters into low-lying villages built on floodplains. When ice dams break up, the force of the rapidly moving ice is sometimes enough to cause severe damage, knocking out bridges, roads, and homes. Ice-dam floods are fairly common in parts of New England, including New Hampshire, Vermont, and Maine. They are also common across much of Alaska and Canada, but the floodplains in these areas tend to be less developed, so the floods pose little hazards to people.

Coastal Storms and Storm Surges

Coastal areas that are affected by *cyclones* and hurricanes are prone to flooding by storm surges associated with these storms. Storm surges are formed by water that is pushed ahead of storms and typically moves on land as exceptionally high tides in front of these severe ocean storms.

Storm surges represent one of the major, most unpredictable hazards to people living along coastlines.

When hurricanes, cyclones, or extratropical lows (also known as coastal storms and nor'easters) form, they rotate, and the low pressure at the centers of the storms raises the water several feet to several tens of feet (< 1–10 m). This extra water moves ahead of the storms as a storm surge that represents an additional height of water above the normal tidal range. The wind from the storms adds further height to the storm surge, with the total height of the storm surge being determined by the length, duration, and direction of wind, plus how low the pressure gets in the center of the storm. The most destructive storm surges are those that strike low-lying communities at high tide, as the effects of the storm surge and the regular astronomical tides are cumulative.

Like many natural catastrophic events, the heights of storm surges to strike a coastline are statistically predictable. If the height of the storm surges is plotted on a semilogarithmic plot, with the height plotted in a linear interval and the frequency (in years) plotted on a logarithmic scale, then a linear slope results. What this means is that statistically some coastal communities can plan for storm surges of certain height to occur about once in a specified interval, typically calculated as every 50, 100, 300, or 500 years, although there is no way to predict when the actual storm surges will occur. It must be remembered that this is long-term statistical average, and that one, two, three or more 500-year events may occur over a relatively short period, but over a long time period the events average out to once every 500 years.

During some hurricanes and coastal storms the greatest destruction and largest number of deaths are associated with inundation by the storm surge. The waters can rise and cover large regions, staying high for many hours during intense storms, drowning victims of low-lying areas, and continuously pounding structures with the waves that move in on top of the storm surges.

STORM SURGES AND BANGLADESH

The area in the world that seems to be hit by the most frequent and most destructive storm surges is Bangladesh. Bangladesh is a densely populated low-lying country sitting mostly at or near sea level between India and Myanmar (Burma). It is a delta environment, built where the Ganges and Brahmaputra Rivers drop their sediment eroded from the Himalayas. Bangladesh is frequently flooded from high river levels, with up to 20 percent of the low-lying country being underwater in any year.

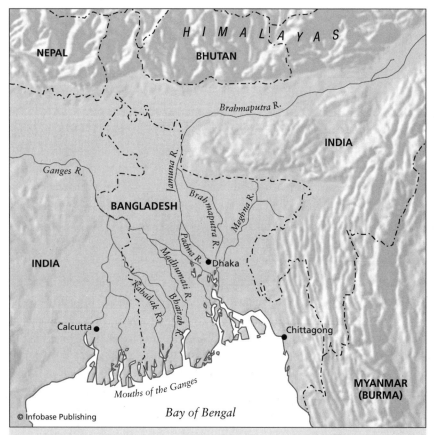

Map of Bangladesh, site of some of the most frequent and devastating floods in the world. Bangladesh sits at the head of the Bay of Bengal and often is hit by typhoons that drive high water in storm surges into the low-lying coastal delta, killing thousands of people. The country is also surrounded by mountains that receive high rainfall and spring snowmelts, bringing floods down the Ganges, Brahmaputra, Jamuna, and Meghna Rivers.

It also sits directly in the path of many Bay of Bengal tropical cyclones (another name for a hurricane) and has been hit by eight of the 10 most deadly tropical cyclone disasters in the history of the world, including Typhoon Sidr in late 2007.

On November 12 and 13, 1970, a category 3 typhoon known as the Bhola cyclone hit Bangladesh with 115 MPH (185 kph) winds and a 23-foot- (7-m-) high storm surge that struck at the astronomically high tides of a full moon. The result was devastating, with about 500,000 human deaths and half a million farm animals perishing. (The death toll is hard to esti- mate in this rural region, with estimates ranging from 300,000 to 1 million people lost in this one storm alone.) Most people and animals perished from flooding associated with the storm surge that covered most of the

A mother and child sit in makeshift home atop a roof in flooded Zinzara, Dhaka, Bangladesh, August 2, 2004. Two and a half million people were displaced from the capital in this flood, and hundreds perished in the fetid waters. *(Reuters, Rafiqur Rahman/Reuters/ Landov)*

low-lying deltaic islands on the Ganges River. The most severely hit area was in Tazmuddin Province, where nearly half the population of 167,000 in the city of Thana was killed by the storm surge. Again in 1990 another cyclone hit the same area, this time with a 20-foot (6-m) storm surge and 145 MPH (233 kph) winds, killing another 140,000 people and another half-million farm animals. In November 2007 Bangladesh was hit by a powerful category 5 cyclone, with 150 MPH (242 kph) winds and was inundated with another 20-foot-high storm surge. Since the 1990 storm the area had a better warning system in place, so many more people evacuated low-lying areas before the storm. Still, it is estimated that 5,000–10,000 people perished during Typhoon Sidr, most from the effects of the storm surge. Nearby Myanmar did not learn this lesson, however, and 134,000 people perished when it was hit by Cyclone Nargis in May 2008.

Flash Floods

Flash floods result from short periods of heavy rainfall and are common near warm oceans, along steep mountain fronts that are in the path of moist winds, and in areas prone to thunderstorms. They are well known in the mountainous areas and canyonlands of the U.S. Southwest and many other parts of the world. Some of the heaviest rainfalls in the United States have occurred along the Balcones escarpment in Texas. Atmospheric instability in this area often forms along the boundary between dry desert air masses to the northwest and warm, moist air masses rising up the escarpment from the Gulf of Mexico to the south and east. Up to 20 inches (0.5 m) of rain have fallen along the Balcones escarpment in as little as three hours from this weather situation. The Balcones escarpment also seems to trap tropical hurricane rains, such as those from Hurricane Alice, which dumped more than 40 inches (102 cm) of rain on the escarpment in 1954. The resulting floodwaters were 65 feet (20 m) deep, one of the largest floods ever recorded in Texas. Approximately 25 percent of the catastrophic flash flooding events in the United States have occurred along the Balcones escarpment. On a slightly longer time scale, tropical hurricanes, cyclones, and monsoonal rains may dump several feet of rain over periods of a few days to a few weeks, resulting in fast but not quite flash flooding.

The national record for the highest, single-day rainfall is held by the south Texas region, when Hurricane Claudette dumped 43 inches (1.1 m) of rain on the Houston area in 1979. The region was hit again by devastating floods on June 8–10, 2001, when an early-season tropical storm suddenly grew off the coast of Galveston and dumped 28–35 inches (0.7–0.9 m) of rain on Houston and surrounding regions. The floods were among the worst in Houston's history, leaving 17,000 people homeless and 22 dead. More than 30,000 laboratory animals died in local hospital and research labs, and the area's many university and hospital research labs experienced hundreds of millions of dollars in damage. Fifty million dollars were set aside to buy out the properties of homeowners who had built on particularly hazardous floodplains. Total damages have exceeded $5 billion and are likely to rise. The standing water left behind by the floods became breeding grounds for disease-bearing mosquitoes, and the humidity led to a dramatic increase in the release of mold spores, which cause allergies in some people, and some of which are toxic.

The Cherrapunji region in southern India at the base of the Himalayas has received the world's highest rainfalls. Moist air masses from the

A flash flood raging down a mountain slope on Maui, Hawaiian Islands *(John Wang/ Getty Images)*

Boulders from a landslide block a road at Grimsel Pass near the village of Guttannen, Switzerland, after heavy rain in August 2005 caused Rotlaui River (upper left) to become engorged and burst its banks. The floods and landslides also caused the nearby Aare River to be diverted, flooding parts of the town of Guttannen. *(Michael Szoenyi/SPL/Photo Researchers, Inc.)*

Bay of Bengal move toward Cherrapunji, where they begin to rise over the high mountains. This produces a strong *orographic effect,* where the air mass cannot hold as much moisture as it rises and cools, so heavy rains result. Cherrapunji has received as much as 30 feet (9 m) of rain in a single month (July 1861) and more than 75 feet (23 m) of rain for all of 1861.

Flash floods typically occur in localized areas where mountains cause atmospheric upwelling leading to the development of huge convective thunderstorms, which can pour several inches of rain per hour onto a mountainous terrain, which in turn focuses the water into steep walled canyons. The result can be frightening, with floodwater raging down canyons as steep, thundering walls of water that crash into and wash away all in their paths. Flash floods can severely erode the landscape in arid and sparsely vegetated regions but do much less to change the landscape.

Many canyons in mountainous regions have fairly large upriver parts of their drainage basins. Sometimes the storm that produces a flash flood with a wall of water may be located so far away that people in the canyon do not even know that it is raining somewhere or that they are in immediate and grave danger. Such was the situation in some of the examples described below.

The severity of a flash flood is determined by a number of factors other than the amount of rainfall. The shape of the drainage basin is important, because it determines how quickly rainfall from different parts of the basin converge at specific points. The soil moisture and previous rain history are important, as are the amounts of vegetation, urbanization, and slope.

BIG THOMPSON CANYON, COLORADO, 1976

Big Thompson Canyon is a popular recreational area located about 50 miles (80 km) northwest of Denver, in the Front Range of the Rocky Mountains. On July 31, 1976, a large thunderhead cloud had grown over the Front Range, and it suddenly produced a huge cloudburst (rainfall) instead of doing the usual thing of blowing eastward over the plains. Approximately 7½ inches (0.2 m) of rain fell in a four-hour period, an

House roof on the bridge over the Big Thompson River near Estes Park, Colorado, August 3, 1976, after the Big Thompson Canyon flood *(AP)*

amount approximately equal to the average yearly rainfall in the area. The steep topography focused the water into Big Thompson Canyon, where a flash flood with a raging 20-foot- (6-m-) high wall of water rushed through the canyon narrows at 15 MPH (24 khr), killing 145 people who were driving into and out of the canyon. As the wall of water roared through the canyon, many people abandoned their cars and scrambled up the canyon walls to safety, only to watch their cars get washed away by the floods. Those people who climbed the canyon walls to escape the flash flood survived, but those who did not or could not perished in the flood. In addition to the deaths this flash flood destroyed 418 homes, 52 businesses, and washed away 400 cars. Damage totals are estimated at $36 million.

FLASH FLOODS IN THE NORTHERN OMAN MOUNTAINS

The Hajar Mountains are a steep rugged range on the northeastern Arabian Peninsula, with deep and long canyons that empty into the Gulf of Oman and Arabian Sea. These normally dry canyons are known as *wadis,* and the local villagers dig wells in the wadi bottoms to reach the groundwater table for use in homes and agriculture. The region is normally very dry, but occasional thunderstorms grow and explode over parts of the mountains. Occasionally a typhoon works its way from the Indian Ocean across the peninsula and may also dump unusual amounts of rain on the mountains. In either situation the canyons become extremely unsafe places to be, and local villagers have tales of flash floods with 100-foot- (30-m-) tall walls of water wiping away entire settlements, leaving only coarse gravel in their place. The inhabitants of this region have learned to place their villages on high escarpments above the wadis, out of the reach of the rare but devastating flash flood. Older destroyed villages are visible in some wadi floors, but the wisdom acquired from experiencing a devastating flash flood has encouraged these people to move to higher ground. The inconvenience of being located 100 feet (30 m) or more above their water source is avoided by building long aqueduct-like structures (known as *falaj*) from water sources located at similar elevations far upstream and letting gravity bring the water to the elevated village site. In August 2007 Typhoon Gonu caused severe flooding across northern Oman, with floods ripping through mountain canyons and inundating the capital streets of Muscat with 5–10 feet (1–3 m) of water. Damage was severe, with many homes damaged, shops destroyed, and people in need of rescue from the desert streets by motorboat.

FLASH FLOODS IN THE SOUTHERN ALPS
AND ALGERIA, 2000 AND 2001

In November 2001 parts of Algeria in North Africa received heavy rainfall over a period of two days that led to the worst flooding and mudslides in the capital city of Algiers in more than 40 years. It is estimated that close to 1,000 people died in Algiers, buried by fast moving *mudflow*s that swept out of the Atlas Mountains to the south and moved through the city, hitting some of the poorest neighborhoods with the worst flooding. The Bab El-Oued district, one of the poorest in Algiers, was hit the worst, where 600 people were buried under mudflows several feet (1 m) thick.

These floods followed similar heavy rains, floods, and mudslides that had devastated parts of southern Europe in October 2000. Northern Italy and Switzerland were among the worst hit areas, where water levels reached their highest levels in 30 years, killing about 50 people.

In Switzerland the southern mountain village of Gondo was devastated when a 120-foot- (37-m-) wide mudflow ripped through the town center, removing 10 homes (one-third of the village) and killing 13 people. Numerous roads, bridges, and railroads were washed away throughout the region, stretching from southern France, through Switzerland and Italy, to the Adriatic Sea. Crops were destroyed on a massive scale. Tens of thousands of people had to be evacuated from throughout the region, and total damage estimates are in the range of many billions of dollars.

Examples of Regional Flood Disasters

Some flooding events are massive in scale, covering hundreds of thousands of acres along the entire floodplain of a river system with water. These floods tend to rise slowly and may have high water for weeks or even months. History has shown that many levees fail during regional long-term flooding events, because most levees are designed to hold back high water for only short amounts of time. As the length of time the water stays high increases, the longer the water pressure acts on the levee, slowly forcing the water into the pores, letting the water seep into and under the levee. This often results in levee failure, explaining why so many levees fail in long-term regional floods. Long-term flooding events can affect hundreds of thousands, or even millions, of people and cause widespread disease, famine, loss of jobs, and displacement of populations as a result of the disaster. Floods of this magnitude are among the costliest of all natural disasters.

MISSISSIPPI RIVER BASIN AND THE U.S. MIDWEST

The Mississippi River is the largest river basin in the United States and the third largest river basin in the world. It is the site of frequent, sometimes devastating floods. All of the 11 major tributaries of the Mississippi River have also experienced major floods, including events that have at least quadrupled the normal river discharge in 1883, 1892, 1903, 1909, 1927, 1973, and 1993. Three of the major rivers (Mississippi, Missouri, and Illinois) meet in St. Louis, which has seen some of the worst flooding along the entire system.

Floods along the Mississippi River in the 18th and 19th centuries prompted the formation of the Mississippi River Commission (MRC), which oversaw the construction of high levees along much of the length of the river from New Orleans to Iowa. By 1926 more than 1,800 miles (2,896 km) of levees had been constructed, many of them more than 20 feet (6 m) tall. The levees gave people a false sense of security against

Satellite views of the St. Louis, Missouri, area, at flood river flow levels (left) in August 1991, and normal levels (right) on August 19, 1993, during the great flood of 1993 (*NASA Earth Observatory, Jesse Allen*)

the floodwaters of the mighty Mississippi. The levees in fact restricted the channel, causing floods to rise more quickly and forcing the water to flow faster.

Many weeks of rain in the late fall of 1926 followed by high winter snowmelts in the upper Mississippi River Basin caused the river to rise to alarming heights by spring 1927. Residents all along the Mississippi were worried and were strengthening and heightening the levees and dikes along the river, hoping to avert disaster. The crest of water was moving through the upper Midwest and had reached central Mississippi, and the rains continued. In April levees began collapsing along the river sending torrents of water over thousands of acres of farmland, destroying homes, drowning livestock, and leaving 50,000 people homeless. One of the worst-hit areas was Washington County, Mississippi, where an intense late April storm dumped an incredible 15 inches (38 cm) of rain in 18 hours, causing additional levees along the river to collapse. One of the most notable was the Mounds Landing levee, whose collapse caused a 10-foot- (3-m-) deep lobe of water to cover the Washington County town of Greenville on April 22. The river reached 50 miles (80 km) in width and had flooded approximately 1 million acres (4,047 km^2), washing away an estimated 2,200 buildings in Washington County alone. Many people perished trying to keep the levees from collapsing and were washed away in the deluge. The floodwaters remained high for more than two months, and people were forced to leave the area (if they could afford to) or to live in refugee camps on the levees, which were crowded and unsanitary. An estimated 1,000 people perished in the floods of 1927, some from the initial flood and more from famine and disease in the months following the inundation by the floodwaters. More than 1 million people were displaced from their homes, and a total of 27,000 square miles (43,450 km²) were flooded. Crop losses amounted to $102.6 million, and 162,000 homes were inundated with floodwaters.

With most tributaries and reservoirs filled to capacity by the end of the summer, 1972 became another wet year along the Mississippi. The rains continued through the winter of 1972–73, and the snowpack thickened over the northern part of the Mississippi River Basin. The combined snowmelts and continued rains caused the river to reach flood levels at St. Louis in early March, before the snow had even finished melting. Heavy rain continued throughout the Mississippi basin and the river continued to rise through April and May, spilling into fields and low-lying areas. The Mississippi was so high that it rose to more than 50 feet above its average levels for much of the lower river basin, and these river heights caused many of the smaller tributaries to back up until they too were at this height. The floodwaters rose to levels not seen for 200 years. At Baton Rouge the river nearly broke through its banks and established a new course to the Gulf of Mexico, which would have left New Orleans without a river.

The floodwaters began peaking in late April, causing 30,000 people to be evacuated in St. Louis by April 28, and close to 70,000 people in the region. The river remained at record heights throughout the lower drainage basin through late June. Damage estimates exceeded $750 million.

In the late summer of 1993 the Mississippi River and its tributaries in the upper basin rose to levels not seen in more than 130 years. The discharge at St. Louis was measured at more than 1 million cubic feet (28,320 m³) per second. The weather situation that led to these floods was remarkably similar to that of the floods of 1927 and 1973, only worse. High winter snowmelts were followed by heavy summer rainfalls caused by a low-pressure trough that stalled over the Midwest, because it was blocked by a stationary high-pressure ridge that formed over the East Coast of the United States. The low-pressure system drew moist air from the Gulf of Mexico that met the cold air from the eastern high-pressure ridge, initiating heavy rains for much of the summer.

The rivers continued to rise until August, when they reached unprecedented flood heights. The discharge of the Mississippi was the highest recorded, and the height of the water was even greater because all the levees that had been built restricted the water from spreading laterally and caused the water to rise more rapidly than it would have without the levees in place. More than two-thirds of all the levees in the upper Mississippi River Basin were breached, overtopped, or damaged by the floods of 1993. Forty-eight people died in the 1993 floods, and 50,000 homes were damaged or destroyed. Total damage costs are estimated at more than $20 billion.

The examples of the floods of 1927 and 1993 on the Mississippi reveal the dangers of building extensive levee systems along rivers. Levees adversely affect the natural processes of the river, and may actually make floods worse. The first effect they have is to confine the river to a narrow channel, causing the water to rise faster than if it were able to spread across its floodplain. Additionally, as the water can no longer flow across the floodplain, it cannot seep into the ground as effectively, and a large amount of water that would normally be absorbed by the ground now must flow through the confined river channel. The floods are therefore larger because of the levees. A third

The flooded Missouri River covers a portion of Hermann, Missouri, July 9, 1993. The first stream of water behind the city is the Missouri River, and the upper two streams are floodwaters from the river. *(AP)*

hazard of levees is associated with their failure. When a levee breaks, it does so with the force of hundreds or thousands of acres of elevated river water pushing it from behind. The force of the water that broke through the Mounds Landing levee in the 1927 flood is estimated to be equivalent to the force of water flowing over the Niagara Falls. If the levees were not in place, the water would have risen gradually and would have been much less catastrophic when it eventually came into the farmlands and towns along the Mississippi River Basin.

The U.S. Army Corps of Engineers is mitigating another hazard and potential disaster where the Atchafalaya branches off the Mississippi. The Mississippi River has over geological time altered its course so that its mouth has migrated east and west by hundreds of miles. Each course of the river has produced its own delta, which subsides below sea level after the river migrates to another location. Subsidence of the delta deposit occurs primarily because the river no longer replenishes the top of the delta, and the buried muds gradually compact as the water is expelled out from the pore spaces by the weight of the overlying sediments. As the delta subsides to sea level, waves add to the erosion, keeping the delta surface below sea level. At the present time the lower Mississippi River follows a long and circuitous course from where the Atchafalaya River branches off from it, past New Orleans, to its mouth near Venice. The Mississippi River is ready to switch its course back to its earlier position, following the Atchafalaya, which would offer it a shorter course to the sea and would take less energy to transport sediment to the Gulf of Mexico. If this were to occur, it would be devastating to the lower delta, which would quickly subside below sea level. The city of New Orleans is currently below sea level and only protected from the river, storms, and the Gulf of Mexico by high levees built around the city. In order to prevent this disaster from occurring, the army corps is constructing an extensive system of diversions, levees, and dams at the Mississippi-Atchafalaya junction with the aim of keeping the Mississippi in its channel.

(opposite) Map of Louisiana showing the present position of the Mississippi, Red, and Atchafalaya Rivers and the present and past positions of the Mississippi River Delta lobes. New Orleans and the active lobe are currently subsiding, and the Mississippi is poised to attempt to find a shorter route to the sea, such as along the Atchafalaya River. The U.S. Army Corps of Engineers is actively monitoring this junction and maintaining levees and other river control structures to prevent the river from switching course.

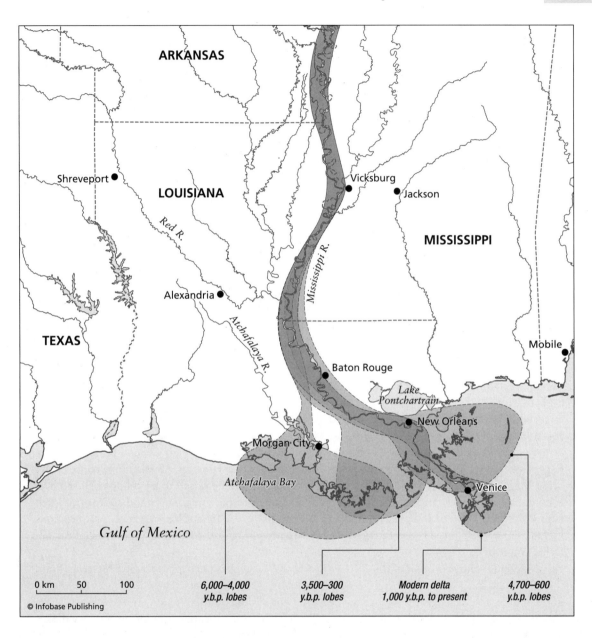

6,000–4,000
y.b.p. lobes

3,500–300
y.b.p. lobes

Modern delta
1,000 y.b.p. to present

4,700–600
y.b.p. lobes

© Infobase Publishing

YELLOW RIVER, CHINA

More people have been killed from floods along the Yellow (Huang) River in China than from any other natural feature, whether river, volcano, fault, or coastline. It is estimated that millions of people have died as a result of floods and famine generated by the Yellow River, which has earned it the nickname of the River of Sorrow in China.

The Yellow River flows out of the Kunlun Mountains across much of China into the wide lowland basin between Beijing and Shanghai. The river has switched courses in its lower reaches at least 10 times in the last 2,500 years. It currently flows into Chihli (Bohai) Bay and then into the Yellow Sea.

The Chinese have attempted to control and modify the course of the Yellow River: Dredging operations were undertaken in 2356 B.C.E., and levees were constructed in 602 B.C.E. One of the worst modern floods along the Yellow River was in 1887, when the river rose over the top of the 75-foot- (22-m-) high levees and covered the lowlands with water. More than 1 million people died from the floods and subsequent famine. Crops and livestock were destroyed, and sorrow returned to the river.

ADOLPHUS A. BUSCH IV: PIONEER OF FLOODPLAIN PRESERVATION

Some people see something wrong with a system and decide to do something about it. Few people have done more to protect America's floodplain environments and ecosystems from devastation by development and the construction of levees than Adolphus A. Busch IV, of the Anheuser-Busch brewing family.

Busch was born in St. Louis, Missouri, on July 17, 1953, went to the University of Denver for two years then graduated from St. Louis University with a degree in business. After graduating, he worked as manager of Grant's Farm in St. Louis then at Drexel Burnham Investment Co. and purchased Silver Eagle Distributing in 1984, selling it three years later to purchase Houston AB Distributorship. He has other business interests in Idaho, Florida, and St. Louis, where he raised three children. Busch is an accomplished bonefish and tarpon fisherman and guide, a former polo player and sponsor of Michelob Polo from 1986 to the present, and active with many wildlife and conservation organizations, including Ducks Unlimited, Great Rivers Habitat Alliance (GRHA), the National Rifle Association, and Delta Waterfowl.

As founder and chairman of the GRHA in St. Louis, Busch has been a pioneer in preserving floodplain habitats and riverways along the Mississippi and Missouri Rivers. The GRHA was founded in 2000 in order to challenge and reduce the development of the floodplains along the two rivers. Under Busch's leadership, this organization has steadfastly sought to educate the public and policy makers about the hazards of developing floodplains and constructing new levees, and has raised the attention about the importance of saving floodplains as natural water storage areas, wildlife habitats, and productive farming communities.

Busch and the GRHA have legally challenged the U.S. Army Corps of Engineers, preventing it from starting individual levee projects designed to promote development on floodplains. More important, GRHA has joined with other conservation groups, including the National Wildlife Federation, to form the Corps Reform Network, aimed at changing the policies of the U.S. Army Corps of Engineers, whose mission is faulty in terms of its quest to modify riverways and promote development on floodplains.

The Yellow River was also the site of a mixed natural and unnatural disaster in 1938. As part of the war effort, in 1938, Chiang Kai-shek is said to have attacked and bombed the levees along the Yellow River to trap the advancing Japanese army. The Japanese had been brutally advancing inland from the coast, and the Chinese adopted a scorched-earth policy, burning towns and villages before retreating, to leave nothing for the Japanese. The war was resulting in more than 1,000 deaths a day for the Japanese, and more for the Chinese, in some of history's largest military battles. When the Japanese army got to Xuzhou, in Jiangsu Province, the area was deserted, and they captured the empty city on May 20, 1938, and were preparing to move further inland. However, torrential rains were causing flooding problems along the Yellow and Yangtze (Chang) Rivers, and progress was slow. Then, in June, the

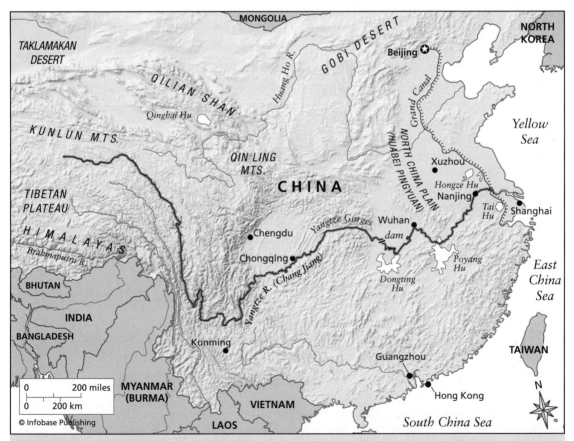

Map of eastern Asia showing the courses of the Yellow (Huang) and Yangtze (Chang) Rivers. The Yellow River has caused some of the deadliest regional floods in recent history, killing more than a million people on two occasions in 1887 and 1938.

levees along the Yellow River were apparently cut (some historians say they broke naturally), and one of the river's greatest floods ensued. The river escaped, initially inundating 500 square miles (1,295 km²) and took another million lives as the flooding spread throughout June and July as the rains continued. The massive floods of the Yellow and Yangtze Rivers forced the Japanese to begin a disorganized retreat in rafts and boats. They again tried to advance up the Yangtze and, with great loss of life, made progress and captured towns up to Jiujiang, in Jiangxi Province. On August 3 the Chinese army cut the dikes on the Yangtze, flooding and killing many more people but effectively ending the two-month-long drive by the Japanese army up the Yangtze. By the middle of August the Japanese were retreating from their drive into central China up the Yangtze, following the floodwaters to sea.

The Yellow River is continuing its natural process of building up its bottom, and the people along the river continue to raise the level of the levees in an attempt to keep the river's floods out of their fields. Today the river bottom rests an astounding 65 feet (20 m) above the surrounding floodplain, a testament to the attempts of the river to find a new lower channel and to abandon its current channel in the process of avulsion. What will happen if heavy rains cause another serious flood along the River of Sorrow? Will another million people perish?

Conclusion

Floods are the costliest, deadliest, and most common natural disaster to affect the human race. Some individual floods have killed on the order of a million people, and other floods cause billions of dollars in damages and ruin entire towns, disrupt livelihoods of hundreds of thousands of people, and bring disease and famine to affected regions.

There are many types of floods, ranging from isolated flash floods that sweep down isolated mountain canyons to coastal floods associated with tropical cyclones and other large ocean storms. Bangladesh has experienced the most frequent and most deadly storm surge–related flooding of anywhere in the world, with some storms killing hundreds of thousands of people. Some of the most devastating floods in history have been large, slowly rising regional floods that cover entire regions, with the Yellow and Yangtze Rivers of China having the dubious distinction of recording the two deadliest floods of all time, each flood claiming more than a million lives. Floods along the Mississippi-Missouri-Ohio River basins in the United States have been frequent and long lasting and have caused great damage to areas on the floodplains that have been built up for commercial or residential uses. Had these areas remained natural, or been used for agriculture, the damages would have been much less, and the river floods would have been lower in magnitude. Construction of levees along these rivers has constricted the rivers with time, raising the base of the river, in turn raising the river flood stages and leading to more disastrous floods.

5

The Groundwater System and Groundwater Contamination

Groundwater is all the water located beneath the Earth's surface, whether it is in the pore spaces between grains of sand and dirt, in large underground caverns, or in small fractures in bedrock. There is about 35 times as much water in the groundwater system as in the surface water system, including all the water in lakes, ponds, streams, rivers, and glaciers. Much of the world's population gets their freshwater from the groundwater system, pumping the water from beneath the surface or pulling buckets up from wells dug into the ground. Any body of rock or unconsolidated sediment that can hold and transmit water is known as an aquifer. Units that restrict the flow of water are known as *aquitards.*

Groundwater comes from rainfall and surface flow, where it seeps into the ground and slowly makes its way downhill toward the sea. There is water everywhere beneath the ground surface, and most of this occurs within 2,500 feet (750 m) of the surface. The volume of groundwater is estimated to be equivalent to a layer 180 feet (55 m) thick spread evenly over the Earth's entire land surface. The distribution of water in the ground can be divided into the unsaturated and the saturated zones. The top of the *water table* is defined as the upper surface of the saturated zone; below this surface, all openings are filled with water.

Increasingly, groundwater is being used for more functions than simply drinking or watering plants and animals. Water has a high specific heat capacity, meaning that it takes a long time and a lot of heat energy to heat up and cool down the water. Additionally, the insulating effects of the surrounding soil and bedrock means that the groundwater tends to remain at a similar temperature year round, in the low 50s Fahrenheit (10–12°C). Using these properties, engineers are beginning to use water to help heat and cool buildings using water. During hot weather the water is pumped through radiators, cooling the building. In cool weather the water is heated, and as water stores heat energy more efficiently than air, energy savings result.

Freshwater is one of the most important resources in the world. Wars have been and will be fought over the ability to obtain freshwater, and water rights are hot political issues in places where it is scarce, such as in the American West and the Middle East. Since we live in a finite world with a finite amount of freshwater, and the global population is growing rapidly, it is likely that freshwater will become an increasingly important topic for generations to come. Much of the groundwater in the world is at increasing risk of being contaminated by industrial and human pollutants, and efforts must be undertaken to adequately protect this scarce resource.

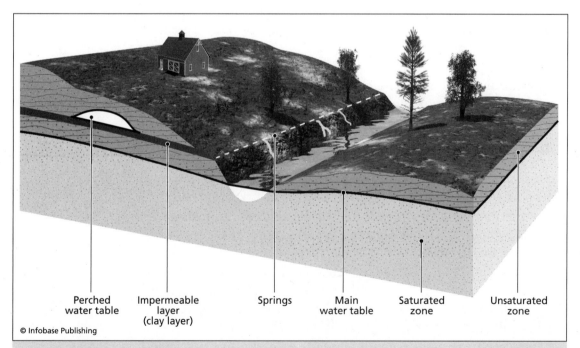

| Perched water table | Impermeable layer (clay layer) | Springs | Main water table | Saturated zone | Unsaturated zone |

© Infobase Publishing

Groundwater system, showing main water table, perched water table above impermeable layer, springs, and saturated and unsaturated zones

The United States and other nations have come to realize that groundwater is a vital resource for a nation's survival and are only recently beginning to appreciate that much of the world's groundwater resources have become contaminated by natural and human-aided processes. Approximately 40 percent of drinking water in the United States comes from groundwater reservoirs. About 80 billion gallons of groundwater are pumped out of these reservoirs every day in the United States.

Movement of Groundwater

Most of the water under the ground does not just sit there; it is constantly in motion, although rates are typically only an inch or two (2–5 cm) per day. The rates of movement are controlled by the amount of open space in the bedrock or *regolith* and how the spaces are connected. The groundwater system also includes water beneath the ground that is immobile, such as water locked up in soil moisture and permafrost, plus geothermal and oil formation water.

Porosity is the percentage of total volume of a body that consists of open spaces. Sands and gravels typically have about 20 percent open spaces, while clays have about 50 percent. The sizes and shapes of grains determine the porosity, which is also influenced by how much they are compacted, cemented together, or deformed.

In contrast, *permeability* is a body's capacity to transmit fluids or to allow the fluids to move through its open pore spaces. Permeability is not directly related to porosity, because if all the pore spaces in a body are isolated, then it may have high porosity, but the water may be trapped and unable to move through the body. Permeability is also affected by *molecular attraction,* the force that makes thin films of water stick to things, instead of being forced to the ground by gravity. If the pore spaces in a material are very small, as in clay, then the force of molecular attraction is strong enough to stop the water from flowing through the body. When the pores are large, the water in the center of the pores is free to move.

After a rainfall, much of the water stays near the surface, because clay in the near-surface horizons of the soil retains much water because of its molecular attraction. This forms a layer of soil moisture in many regions and is able to sustain seasonal plant growth.

Some of this near-surface water evaporates, and plants use some of the near-surface water. Other water runs directly off into streams. The remaining water seeps into the saturated zone or into the water table. Once in the saturated zone it moves by percolation, gradually and slowly, from high areas to low areas under the influence of gravity. These lowest areas are usually lakes or streams. Many streams form where the water table intersects the surface of the land.

Once in the water table, the paths that individual particles follow vary; the transit time from surface to stream may vary from days to thousands of years along a single hillside. Water can flow upward because of high pressure at depth and low pressure in the stream.

The Groundwater System

Groundwater is best thought of as a system of many different parts. Some of these act as conduits and reservoirs, and others, as entrances and exits into the groundwater system.

Recharge areas are where water enters the groundwater system, and *discharge areas* are where water leaves the groundwater system. In humid climates recharge areas encompass nearly the entire land surface,

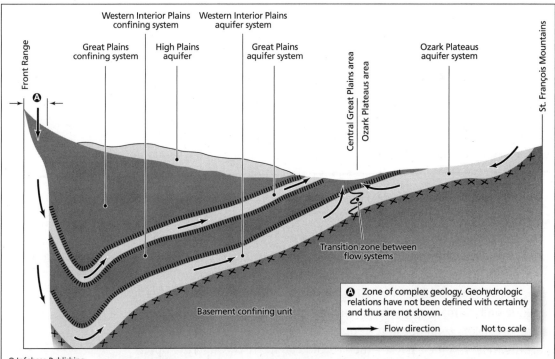

© Infobase Publishing

Regional aquifer system of the Central Plains of the United States showing confined and unconfined aquifers, driven by higher topography in the west

except for streams and floodplains, whereas in desert climates recharge areas consist mostly of the mountains and alluvial fans. Discharge areas consist mostly of streams and lakes. Many aquifer systems extend across vast regions. For instance, the Midwest and Plains states region of the United States is underlain by regional aquifers that include the shallow-level High Plains aquifers, then some deeply buried aquifers, including the Great Plains aquifer system, and the Western Interior Plains aquifer system. The latter two aquifers are confined between *aquicludes,* and since their western margins are at much higher elevations than their eastern sides, the water tapped from these systems can be under high *artesian pressure.*

Drilling a groundwater well *(Shutterstock)*

The level of the water table changes with different amounts of precipitation. In humid regions it reflects the topographic variation, whereas in dry times or places, it tends to flatten out to the level of the streams of lakes. Water flows faster when the slope is greatest, so groundwater flows faster during wet times. The fastest rate of groundwater flow yet observed in the United States is 800 feet (250 m) per year.

Most wells fill with water simply because they intersect the water table. However, the rocks below the surface are not always homogeneous, which can result in a complex type of water table known as a *perched water table.* These result from discontinuous bodies in the subsurface, which create bodies of water at elevations higher than the main water table.

Aquifers

Aquifers are any body of permeable rock or regolith saturated with water through which groundwater moves. The term *aquifer* is usually reserved for rock or soil bodies that contain economical quantities of water that are extractable by existing methods. The quality of an aquifer depends on two main quantities, porosity and permeability. Porosity is a measure of the total amount of open void space in the material. Permeability refers to the ease at which a fluid can move through the open pore spaces and depends in part on the size, shape, and how connected individual pore spaces are in the material. Gravels and sandstone make good aquifers, as do fractured rock bodies. Clay is so impermeable that it makes bad aquifers and typically forms aquicludes, which stop the movement of water.

There are several main types of aquifers. In uniform permeable rock and soil masses, aquifers will form as a uniform layer below the water table. In these simple situations wells fill with water simply because they intersect the water table. However, the rocks below the surface are not always homogeneous and uniform, which can result in a complex type of water table known as a perched water table. These result from discontinuous impermeable rock or soil bodies in the subsurface, which create domed pockets of water at elevations higher than the main water table, resting on top of the impermeable layer.

When the upper boundary of the groundwater in an aquifer is the water table, the aquifer is said to be unconfined. In many regions a permeable layer, typically a sandstone, is confined between two impermeable beds, creating a confined aquifer. In these systems water only enters the system in a small recharge area, and if this is in the mountains, then the aquifer may be under considerable pressure. This is known as an artesian system. Water that escapes the system from the fracture or well reflects the pressure difference between the elevation of the source area and the discharge area (*hydraulic gradient*) and rises above the aquifer as an artesian spring, or artesian well. Some of these wells have made

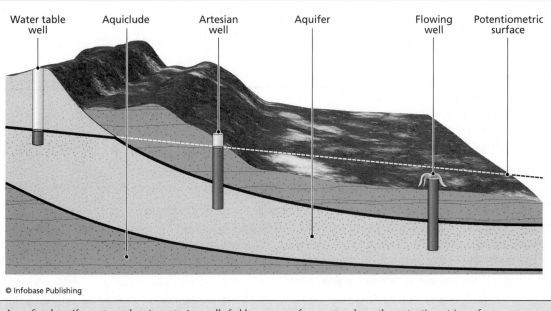

© Infobase Publishing

A confined aquifer system, showing artesian wells fed by pressure from water above the potentiometric surface

fountains that have spewed water 200 feet (60 m) high. One example of an artesian system is that in Florida, where water enters in the recharge area and is released near Miami about 19,000 years later.

Groundwater also reacts chemically with the surrounding rocks; it may deposit minerals and cement together grains, causing a reduction in porosity and permeability, or form features such as *stalagtites* and *stalagmites* in caves. In other cases, particularly when water moves through limestone, it may dissolve the rock, forming caves and underground tunnels. Where these dissolution cavities intersect the surface of the Earth, they form *sinkholes.*

FRACTURE ZONE AQUIFERS

It has become increasingly appreciated that significant quantities of freshwater are stored in fractures within otherwise impermeable crystalline rocks beneath the ground. Many buried granite and other bedrock bodies are cut by many fractures, faults, and other cracks, some of which may have open spaces along them. Fractures at various scales represent zones of increased porosity and permeability. They may form networks and therefore are able to store and carry vast amounts of water. These types of groundwater systems are *fracture zone aquifers,* and are similar in some ways to karst systems.

The concept of fracture zone aquifers explains the behavior of groundwater in large fault-controlled watersheds. Fault zones in this case serve as collectors and transmitters of water from one or more recharge zones, with surface and subsurface flow being strongly controlled by regional fault patterns.

Both the yield and quality of water in these zones are usually higher than average wells in any type of rock. High-grade water for such a region would be 250 gallons (950 l) per minute or greater. In addition, the total dissolved solids measured in the water from such high-yielding wells will be lower than the average for the region.

The quality and amount of water obtainable from fracture zone aquifers are influenced by the pattern of fractures and their related secondary porosity over an entire watershed area. It is important to understand how the fracture pattern varies across a basin to be able to determine the unique effects of secondary porosity on the processes of groundwater flow, infiltration, *transmissivity,* and storage, and ultimately find and use the water in the fractures.

Variations in precipitation over the catchment area can determine how a fracture zone aquifer system is recharged. One example

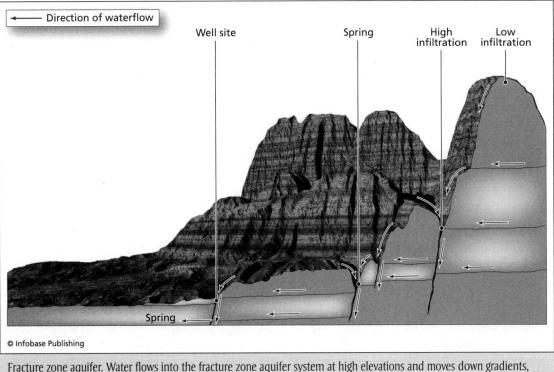

Fracture zone aquifer. Water flows into the fracture zone aquifer system at high elevations and moves down gradients, where it may be stored in deep fractures beneath alluvium.

is orographic effects where the precipitation over the mountains is substantially greater than at lower elevations. The rainfall is collected over a large catchment area, which contains zones with high permeability because of intense bedrock fracturing associated with major fault zones. The multitude of fractures within these highly permeable zones "funnels" the water into other fracture zones down gradient. These funnels may be in a network hundreds of square miles in area.

The fault and fracture zones serve as conduits for groundwater and often act as channelways for surface flow. Intersections form rectilinear drainage patterns that are sometimes exposed on the surface but are also represented below the surface and converge down gradient. In some regions these rectilinear patterns are not always visible on the surface due to vegetation and sediment cover. The convergence of these groundwater conduits increases the amount of water available as recharge. The increased permeability, water volume, and ratio of water to minerals within these fault-fracture zones help to maintain the quality of water supply. These channels occur in fractured, nonporous media (crystalline rocks) as well as in fractured, porous media (sandstone, limestone).

At some point in the groundwater course, after convergence, the gradient decreases. The sediment cover over the major fracture zone becomes thicker and acts as a water storage unit with primary porosity. The major fracture zone acts as both a transmitter of water along conduits and a water storage basin along connected zones with secondary (and/or primary) porosity. Groundwater within this layer or lens often flows at accelerated rates. The result can be a pressurization of groundwater both in the fracture zone and in the surrounding material. Rapid flow in the conduit may be replenished almost instantaneously from precipitation. The surrounding materials are replenished more slowly but also release the water more slowly and serve as a storage unit to replenish the conduit between precipitation events.

Once the zones are saturated, any extra water that flows into them will overflow, if an exit is available. In a large area watershed it is likely

LOVE CANAL AND THE SUPERFUND ACT

Love Canal is not a place many people would choose to visit on a honeymoon. Love Canal was a quiet neighborhood in Niagara Falls, New York, that became infamous for being one of the most horrific toxic waste dumps in the country. The history of Love Canal began in the 1890s, when an entrepreneur named William T. Love envisioned building a canal that would connect the two levels of the Niagara River, above and below the falls, for generating electricity and eventually as a shipping canal. He dug about a mile (1.6 km) of the canal, with a channel about 15 feet (5 m) wide and 10 feet (3 m) deep, before his scheme failed and the project was abandoned. Eventually his land was sold to the city of Niagara Falls, which used the undeveloped land as a landfill for chemical waste. The canal was thought to be appropriate for this use because the geology consisted of impermeable clay and the area was rural. The area was then acquired by Hooker Chemical, which continued its use as a toxic chemical landfill and dumped more than 22,000 tons (19,954 tonnes) of toxic waste into the site from 1942 to 1952, until the canal was full. Then the site was backfilled with four feet (1.2 m) of clay and closed.

As the city of Niagara Falls expanded, land was needed for many purposes, including schools. The local school board attempted to buy the land from Hooker Chemical, but the chemical company initially refused, showing the school board that the site was a toxic waste dump. The school board eventually won and was able to purchase the site for $1, with a release to Hooker Chemical that the company explained to them about the toxic wastes below the surface and that they would not be liable for deaths or health problems resulting from the waste. A school was then built directly on top of the toxic landfill, and during construction, the contractors broke through the clay seal under the landfill that had been placed there to prevent leakage of the waste into the local groundwater system. Soon after this, in 1957 the city constructed sewers for a neighborhood growing around the school, and in doing so broke through the seal of the landfill again, and chemicals began seeping out of the old canal in more locations. Further construction of roads in the area restricted some of

that this water flows along subsurface channelways under pressure until some form of exit is found in the confining environment. Substantial amounts of groundwater may flow along the main fault zone controlling the watershed and may vent at submarine extensions of the fault zone forming coastal or offshore freshwater springs.

Fracture zone aquifers are most common in areas underlain by crystalline rocks and where these rocks have undergone a multiple deformational history that includes several faulting events. It is especially applicable in areas where recharge is possible from seasonal and/or sporadic rainfall on mountainous regions adjacent to flat desert areas.

Fracture zone aquifers are distinguished from horizontal alluvial or sedimentary formation aquifers in various ways: 1) They drain extensive areas and many extend for tens of miles (several tens of km) in length; 2) they constitute conduits to mountainous regions where the recharge potential from rainfall is high; 3) some may connect several horizontal aquifers and thereby increase the volume of accumulated water;

---

the groundwater flow, and water levels in the old canal rose above ground level, so the site became an elongate pond.

Children in the area began showing health problems, including epilepsy, asthma, and infections, but the source was not known. In 1978 parents in the community united under the leadership of a concerned mother named Lois Gibbs and discovered that their community was built on top of a huge toxic waste dump. Their complaints of sick children, chemical odors, and strange substances oozing out of the ground were at first ignored by local officials but were heard in 1979 by the Environmental Protection Agency (EPA). The EPA documented a disturbingly high incidence of miscarriages, nervous disorders, cancers, and strange birth defects. More than half of the children born in Love Canal between 1974 and 1978 were documented to have birth defects, some of which were severe. Many legal and political battles ensued, with the residents unable to sell their homes, the city and Hooker Chemical (by that time a subsidiary of Occidental Petroleum) denying liability, and the health problems persisting. The residents were losing the legal battles against the local government and the big chemical company.

On August 7, 1978, President Jimmy Carter declared a federal emergency at Love Canal and began relocating residents closest to the canal. Carcinogens such as benzene were discovered in the groundwater around the site, and many residents were showing a range of severe health effects, including leukemia. On May 21, 1980, President Carter declared a wider state of emergency and ended up relocating more than 800 families away from the site. This, and a similar chemical waste catastrophe at Times Beach, Missouri, led Congress to pass the Comprehensive Environmental Response, Compensation, and Liability Act (CERCLA), commonly known as the Superfund Act. Occidental Petroleum was sued by the EPA, and it paid $129 million in compensation. A permanent Superfund Act has helped hold many polluters liable for similar negligent acts that have polluted the nation's land and groundwater resources since that time.

4) because the source of the water is at higher elevations, the artesian pressure at the groundwater level may be high; and 5) they are usually missed by conventional drilling because the water is often at the depth of hundreds of meters.

The characteristics of fracture zone aquifers make them an excellent source of groundwater in arid and semi-arid environments. Fracture zone aquifers are being increasingly used in arid regions. It must be recognized that groundwater resources in arid and semi-arid lands are scarce and must be properly used and thoughtfully managed. Most of these resources are "fossil," having accumulated under wet climates during the geological past. The present rates of recharge from the occasional rainfall are not enough to replenish the aquifers; therefore, the resources must be used sparingly without exceeding the optimum pumping rates for each water well field.

Groundwater Contamination

Natural groundwater is typically rich in dissolved elements and compounds derived from the soil, regolith, and bedrock that the water has migrated through. Some of these dissolved elements and compounds are poisonous, whereas others are tolerable in small concentrations but harmful in high concentrations. Groundwater is also increasingly becoming contaminated by human and industrial waste. Furthermore, the overuse of groundwater resources has caused groundwater levels to drop and led to other problems, especially along coastlines. Seawater may move in to replace depleted freshwater, and the ground surface may subside when the water is removed from the pore spaces in aquifers.

The U.S. Public Health Service has established limits on the concentrations of dissolved substances, called "total dissolved solids" (t.d.s.), in natural water that is destined for domestic and other uses. The following table lists these standards for the United States. It should be emphasized that many other countries, particularly those with chronic water shortages, have much more lenient standards. Sweet water is preferred for domestic use and has less than 500 milligrams (mg) of t.d.s. per liter (l) of water. Fresh and slightly saline water with t.d.s. of 1,000–3,000 mg/l is suitable for use by livestock and for irrigation. Water with higher concentrations is unfit for humans or livestock. Irrigation of fields using waters with high concentrations of t.d.s. is also not recommended, as the water will evaporate but leave the dissolved salts and minerals behind, degrading and eventually destroying the productivity of the land.

The quality of groundwater can be reduced or considered contaminated by either a high amount of t.d.s. or by the introduction of a specific toxic element. Most of the t.d.s. in groundwater are salts that have been derived from dissolution of the local bedrock or soils derived from the bedrock. Salts may also seep into groundwater supplies from the sea along coastlines, particularly if the water is being pumped out for use. In these cases seawater often moves in to replace the depleted freshwater.

Dissolved salts in groundwater commonly include the bicarbonate (HCO_3) and sulfate (SO_4) ions, often attached to other ions. Dissolved calcium (Ca) and magnesium (Mg) ions can cause the water to become "hard." Hard water is defined as containing more than 120 parts per million dissolved calcium and magnesium. It is difficult to lather with soap in hard water, which also causes a crusty mineralization to build up on faucets and pipes. Adding sodium (Na) in a water softener can soften hard water, but people with heart problems or those who are on a low-salt diet should not do this. Hard water is common in areas where the groundwater has moved through limestone or dolostone rocks, which contain high concentrations of Ca- and Mg-rich rocks that are easily dissolved by groundwater.

Groundwater may have many other contaminants, some natural and others that are the result of human activity. Human pollutants, including animal and human waste, pesticides, industrial solvents, road salts, petroleum products, and other chemicals, are a serious problem in many areas. Some of the biggest and most dangerous sources of groundwater contamination include chemical and gasoline storage

Drinking Water Standards for the United States	
WATER CLASSIFICATION	TOTAL DISSOLVED SOLIDS
Sweet	< 500 mg/l
Fresh	500–1,000 mg/l
Slightly saline	1,000–3,000 mg/l
Moderately saline	3,000–10,000 mg/l
Very saline	10,000–35,000 mg/l
Brine	> 35,000 mg/l

tanks, septic systems, landfills, hazardous waste sites, military bases, and the general widespread use of road salt and chemicals such as fertilizers as pesticides.

The EPA has led the cleanup from spills from leaking chemical storage tanks in the United States. There are estimated to be more than 10 million buried chemical storage tanks in the United States, containing chemicals such as gasoline, oil, and hazardous chemicals. These tanks can leak over time, and many of the older ones have needed to be replaced in the past two decades, bringing in a new generation of tanks that should last longer and corrode less.

Home and commercial septic systems pose serious threats to some groundwater systems. Most are designed to work effectively and harmlessly, but some were not installed properly or were poorly designed. In many cases groundwater supplies have been contaminated by chemicals

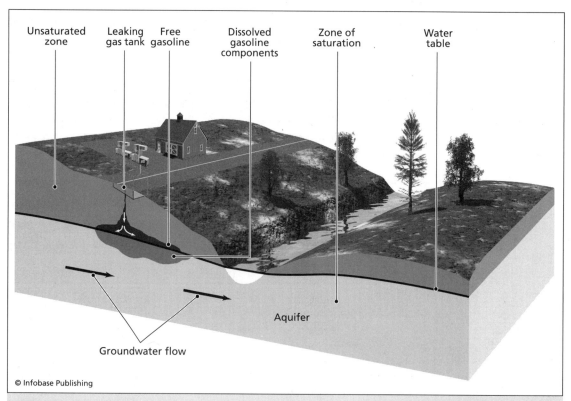

© Infobase Publishing

Gas stations and other industrial sites have leaked hazardous chemicals such as petroleum and gasoline into the ground in many places in the United States, and some of this has worked its way into the groundwater system. Organic liquids (such as gasoline) are lighter than water and tend to float on the top of the water table and work their way down gradient along with the groundwater flow.

Workers remove a 10,000-gallon underground gas storage tank to replace it with a new tank at a gas station in Sacramento, California, May 23, 2003.

and other contaminants that were poured down drains, entering the septic system and then the groundwater system.

There are more than 20,000 known and abandoned hazardous waste sites in the United States. Some of these contain many barrels of chemicals and hazardous materials that can and do leak, contaminating the water supply. Landfills may also contain many hazardous chemicals. When landfills are designed, they are supposed to incorporate a protective impermeable bottom layer to prevent chemicals from entering the groundwater system; however, some chemicals that are erroneously placed in the landfill sometimes burn holes in the basal layer, making their way (with a myriad of other chemicals) into the groundwater system.

In parts of the country that freeze, road salts are commonly used to reduce the amount of ice on the roads. These salts get dissolved by rain water and can eventually make their way down into the aquifers as well, potentially turning an aquifer salty. Together with chemicals from lawn and farm field fertilization and application of pesticides, the amount of these chemicals starts to become significant for the safety of the water quality below ground.

Groundwater contamination, whether natural or human induced, is a serious problem because of the importance of the limited water supply. Pollutants in the groundwater system do not simply wash away with the next rain, as many dissolved toxins in the surface water system do. Groundwater pollutants typically have a *residence time,* or average length of time that it remains in the system, of hundreds or thousands of years. Many groundwater systems are capable of cleaning themselves from natural biological contaminants using bacteria, but other chemical contaminants have longer residence times.

Arsenic in Groundwater

In parts of the world many people have become sick from arsenic dissolved in the groundwater. Arsenic poisoning leads to a variety of horrific diseases, including hyperpigmentation (abundance of red freckles), hyperkeratosis (scaly lesions on the skin), cancerous lesions on the skin, and squamous cell carcinoma. Arsenic may be introduced into the food chain and body in several ways. In Guizhou Province, China, villagers dry their chili peppers indoors over coal fires. Unfortunately, the coal is rich in arsenic (containing up to 35,000 parts per million arsenic), and much of this arsenic is transferred to the chili peppers during the drying process. Thousands of the local villagers are now suffering arsenic poisoning, with cancers and other forms of the disease ruining families and entire villages.

Most naturally occurring arsenic is introduced into the food chain through drinking contaminated groundwater. Arsenic in groundwater is commonly formed by the dissolution of minerals from weathered rocks and soils. In Bangladesh and West Bengal, India, 25–75 million people are at risk for arsenosis because of high concentrations of natural arsenic on groundwater.

Since 1975 the maximum allowable level of arsenic in drinking water in the United States has been 50 parts per billion. The EPA has been considering adopting new standards on the allowable levels of arsenic in drinking water. Scientists from the National Academy recommend that the allowable levels of arsenic be lowered to 10 parts per billion, but this level was overruled by the administration of President George W. Bush. The issue is cost: The EPA estimates that it would cost businesses and taxpayers $181 million per year to bring arsenic levels to the proposed 10 parts per billion level, although some private foundations suggest that this estimate is too low by a factor of three. They estimate that the cost would be passed on to the consumer, and residential water bills would quadruple. The EPA estimates that the health benefits from such a lowering of arsenic levels would prevent between seven and 33 deaths from arsenic-related bladder and lung cancers per year. These issues reflect a delicate and difficult choice for the government. The

A Bangladeshi man shows his hands affected by arsenic contamination in Sonargaon, Bangladesh, June 3, 2003. *(Rafiqur Rahman/Reuters/Landov)*

EPA tries to "maximize health reduction benefits at a cost that is justified by the benefits." How much should be spent to save 7–33 lives per year? Would the money be better spent elsewhere?

Arsenic is not concentrated evenly in the groundwater system of the United States or anywhere else in the world. The U.S. Geological Survey issued a series of maps in 2000 showing the concentration of arsenic in tens of thousands of groundwater wells in the United States. Arsenic is concentrated most in the southwestern part of the United States, with a few peaks elsewhere, such as southern Texas, parts of Montana (due to mining operations), and in parts of the upper Plains states. Perhaps a remediation plan that attacks the highest concentrations of arsenic would be the most cost-effective plan that has the highest health benefit.

Contamination by Sewage

A major problem in groundwater contamination is sewage, typically coming from leaks in sewer lines. If coliform bacteria or other contaminants from sewage get into the groundwater, the aquifer is not usable, and care must be taken and samples analyzed before water is used for drinking.

Human feces is composed of about 25 percent bacteria, consisting mostly of lactobacilli and yeasts in addition to *Escherichia coli, B. fragilis, B. oralis, B. melaninogenicus, Bifidobacterium, Lactobacillus, Clostridium perfringens, Eubacterium, Trichomonas hominis, Salmonella,* and *Entamoeba histolytica.* These bacteria produce acids that are so powerful that they can dissolve the concrete pipes that sewer lines are made from, and they can cause strongly acidic conditions in sanitary sewer lines. In concrete pipes the bacteria produce hydrogen sulfide in condensation above the fluid level in the pipes, which is then oxidized to form sulfuric acid. This sulfuric acid then attacks the pipes, eating away a hole to the exterior and causing cracks in the pipe through which the sewage then leaks into the surrounding soil.

Other compounds are also commonly found in sewage and pose dangers to groundwater supplies. Grease and other kitchen refuse disposed down the drain makes it into the sewer lines and can then leak from the cracks created by the sulfuric acid. Sewers also commonly contain quantities of organic compounds, including dishwashing soap, pesticides, oils, dry cleaning solvents, and prescription drugs. Toxic metals, including lead, copper, zinc, manganese, iron, and tin, are also common in sewage, some from human wastes and others from deteriorating pipes.

Once in the soil system, these waste products are transported by groundwater by several mechanisms. In the process of adsorption, some of the contaminants adhere to soil particles and are transported with the soil in moving groundwater to a new location. Contaminants transported by advection move at the seepage velocity with the bulk flow of the groundwater, moving down the gradient from the source. Contaminants may move by diffusion, a molecular-scale mass transport process where the contaminants move from an area of high gradient area to a lower gradient area. Finally, the contaminants may move by dispersing or mixing with groundwater, or may be altered by biodegradation.

In areas that have been contaminated by sewage, it is possible to remedy the damage through a combination of physical, chemical, and biological treatments. Remediation by physical means typically includes making barriers or interceptor systems and changes to the surface water flow to minimize infiltration in areas that would promote transports of the contaminants. Chemical and biological treatments can be applied to neutralize or consume the contaminants. In many cases, sand filtering can remove bacteria, and aquifers contaminated by coliform bacteria and other human waste can be cleaned more easily than aquifers contaminated by many other elemental and mineral toxins.

Conclusion

Most of the world's freshwater is locked up in glaciers or ice caps, and about 25 percent of the freshwater is stored in the groundwater system. Water in the groundwater system is constantly but slowly moving, being recharged by rain and snow that infiltrates the system, and discharging in streams, lakes, springs, and extracted from wells. Water that moves through a porous network forms aquifers, and underground layers that restrict flow are known as aquicludes. Fracture zone aquifers consist of generally nonpermeable and nonporous crystalline rock units, but faults and fractures that cut the rock create new or secondary porosity along the fractures. If exposed to the surface, these fractures may become filled with water and serve as excellent sources of water in dry regions.

The groundwater system is threatened by pollutants that range from naturally dissolved but deadly elements such as arsenic and sewage to industrial wastes and petroleum products that have leaked from underground storage containers, or were carelessly dumped. Some chemical elements have a short residence time in the groundwater system and are effectively cleaned before long, but other elements may last years or thousands of years before the groundwater is drinkable.

6

Geological Subsidence, Compaction, and Collapse

Natural geologic subsidence is the sinking of land relative to sea level or some other uniform surface. Subsidence may be a gradual, barely perceptible process, or it may occur as a catastrophic collapse of the surface. Subsidence occurs naturally along some coastlines, and it occurs in areas where groundwater has dissolved cave systems in rocks such as limestone. It may occur on a regional scale, affecting an entire coastline, or it may be local in scale, such as when a sinkhole suddenly opens and collapses in the middle of a neighborhood. Other subsidence events reflect the interaction of humans with the environment and include ground surface subsidence as a result of mining excavations, groundwater and petroleum extraction, and several other processes. *Compaction* is a related phenomenon in which the pore spaces of a material are gradually reduced, condensing the material by expelling the water between the grains and causing the surface to subside. Subsidence and compaction do not typically result in death or even injury, but they do cost Americans alone tens of millions of dollars per year. The main hazard of subsidence and compaction is damage to property.

Subsidence and compaction directly affect millions of people. Residents of New Orleans live below sea level and are constantly struggling with the consequences of living on a slowly subsiding delta. Coastal residents in the Netherlands have constructed massive dike systems to try to keep the North Sea out of their slowly subsiding land. The Italian city of Venice has dealt with subsidence caused by groundwater extraction in a uniquely charming way, drawing tourists from around the world. Millions of people live below the high-tide level in Tokyo. The coastline of Texas along the Gulf of Mexico is slowly subsiding, placing residents of Baytown and other Houston suburbs close to sea level and in danger of hurricane-induced storm surges and other more frequent flooding events. In Florida, sinkholes have episodically opened up and swallowed homes and businesses, particularly during times of drought. This chapter examines the causes of this sinking of the land and where subsidence is most and least likely to occur.

The driving force of subsidence is gravity, with the style and amount of subsidence controlled by the physical properties of the soil, pore water, regolith, groundwater, and bedrock underlying the area that is subsiding. Subsidence does not require a transporting medium, but it is aided by other processes such as groundwater dissolution that can remove mineral material and carry it away in solution, creating underground caverns that are prone to collapse. Many subsidence problems are related to changes in the position of the groundwater table, loss of water in cave systems, and extraction of water from the saturated zone or from the areas between individual mineral grains.

Types of Surface Subsidence and Collapse

Some subsidence occurs because of processes that happen at depths of thousands of feet beneath the surface and is referred to as deep subsidence. Other subsidence is caused by shallow near-surface processes and is known as shallow subsidence. Tectonic subsidence is a result of the movement of the plates on a lithospheric scale, whereas human-induced subsidence refers to cases where the activities of people, such as extraction of fluids from depth, have resulted in lowering of the land surface.

Compaction-related subsidence may be defined as the slow sinking of the ground surface because of reduced pore space caused by fluid extraction, lowered pore pressure, and other processes that cause the regolith to become more condensed and occupy a smaller volume. Most subsidence and compaction mechanisms are slow and result in gradual sinking of the land's surface, although sometimes the process may occur catastrophically and is known as collapse.

Carbonate Dissolution and Sinkholes

The formation and collapse of sinkholes is one of the more dramatic deep subsidence mechanisms. Sinkholes form over rock that is readily

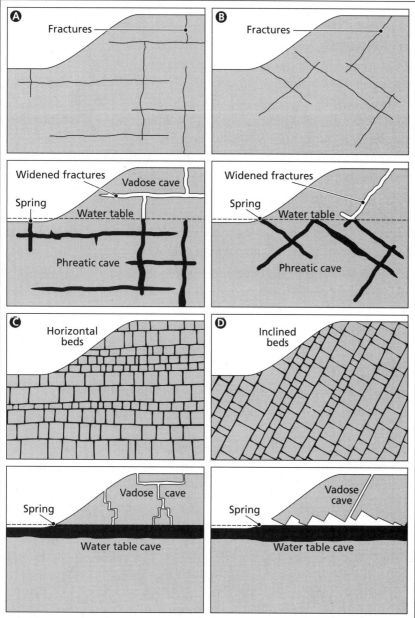

Development of karst caverns along fractures that have been widened by dissolution by groundwater. In (A) sets of vertical and horizontal fractures (upper panel) are widened by dissolution by groundwater (lower panel) forming networks of caves with horizontal chambers and vertical passages, and springs where the caves intersect the ground surface. In (B) the initial fractures (upper panel) are inclined, resulting in inclined cave networks. In (C) caves develop by dissolution along initially horizontal beds, forming horizontal caves and vertical passages with flat roofs, and in (D) initially dipping beds cause the dissolution to occur along dipping planes, and for the roofs of caves to be jagged where different beds are dissolved differentially.

dissolved by *chemical weathering* and groundwater dissolution, and these rocks are most typically limestones. In the United States limestone dissolution and sinkhole formation are an important and dangerous process in Florida, much of the Appalachian Mountains, large parts of the Midwest, scattered areas in and east of the Rocky Mountains, and especially Missouri and northern Arkansas. Areas that are affected by groundwater dissolution, cave complexes, and sinkhole development are known as *karst terrains.* Globally, several regions are known for spectacular karst systems, such as the cave systems of the Caucasus; southern Arabia, including Oman and Yemen; Borneo; and the mature highly eroded karst terrain of southern China's Guangxi region.

The formation of caves and sinkholes in karst regions begins with a process of dissolution. Rainwater that filters through soil and rock may work its way into natural fractures or breaks in the rock, and chemical reactions that remove ions from the limestone slowly dissolve and carry away in solution parts of the limestone. Fractures are gradually enlarged, and new passageways are created by groundwater flowing in underground stream networks through the rock. Dissolution of rocks is most effective if the rocks are limestone and if the water is slightly acidic (acid rain greatly helps cave formation). Carbonic acid (H_2CO_3) in rainwater reacts with the limestone, rapidly (at typical rates of a few millimeters per 1,000 years) creating open spaces, cave and tunnel systems, and interconnected underground stream networks.

When the initial openings become wider, they are known as caves. Many caves are small pockets along enlarged or widened cavities, whereas others are huge, open underground spaces. The largest cave in the world is the Sarawak Chamber in Borneo. This cave has a volume of 65 million cubic feet (1.84 million m³). The Majlis Al Jinn (Khoshilat Maqandeli) Cave in Oman is the second-largest cave known in the world and is big enough to hold several of the sultan of Oman's royal palaces with a 747 flying overhead. Its main chamber is more than 13 million cubic feet (368,000 m³) in volume, larger than the biggest pyramid at Giza. Other large caves include the Belize Chamber, Salle de la Verna, and the largest "Big Room" of the Carlsbad Caverns, New Mexico. Each of these has a volume of at least 3 million cubic feet (85,000 m³). The Big Room is a large chamber 4,000 feet (1,200 m) long, 625 feet (190 m) wide, and 325 feet (100 m) high. Some caves form networks of linked passages that extend for many miles in length. For instance, Mammoth Cave in Kentucky has at least 300 miles (483 km) of interconnected passageways. While the caves are forming, water flows through these passageways in underground stream networks.

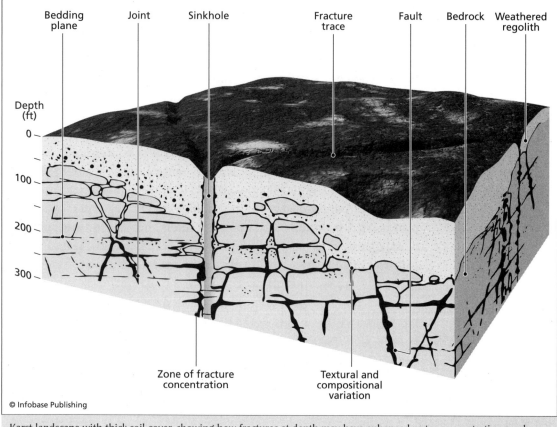

| Bedding plane | Joint | Sinkhole | | Fracture trace | Fault | Bedrock | Weathered regolith |

Depth (ft)
0
100
200
300

Zone of fracture concentration

Textural and compositional variation

© Infobase Publishing

Karst landscape with thick soil cover, showing how fractures at depth may have enhanced water concentrations and leave traces on surfaces as linear valleys. Sinkholes may develop over areas of collapse or loss of material to the cave system at depth.

In many parts of the world the formation of underground cave systems has led to parts of the surface collapsing into the caverns and tunnels, forming a distinctive type of topography known as karst topography. The name *karst* comes from the Kars limestone plateau region in Serbia (the northwest part of the former Yugoslavia), where karst is especially well developed. Karst topography may take on many forms in different stages of landscape evolution but typically begins with the formation of circular pits on the surface known as sinkholes. These form when the roof of an underground cave or chamber suddenly collapses, bringing everything on the surface suddenly down into the depths of the cave. Striking examples of sinkhole formation surprised residents of the Orlando region in Florida in 1981, when a series of sinkholes swallowed many businesses and homes with little warning. In this and many other examples sinkhole formation is initiated after a prolonged drought or drop in the groundwater levels. This drains the water out of underground cave networks, leaving the roofs of chambers unsupported and making them prone to collapse.

The sudden formation of sinkholes in the Orlando area is best illustrated by the formation of the Winter Park sinkhole on May 8, 1981. The first sign that trouble was brewing was provided by the unusual spectacle of a tree suddenly disappearing into the ground at 7:00 P.M. as if being sucked in by some unseen force. Residents were worried, and rightfully so. Within 10 hours a huge sinkhole nearly 100 feet (30 m) across and more than 100 feet (30 m) deep had formed. It continued to grow, swallowing six commercial buildings, a home, two streets, six Porsches, and the municipal swimming pool, causing more than $2 million in damage. The sinkhole has since been converted into a municipal park and lake. More than 1,000 sinkholes have formed in parts of southern Florida in recent years.

Sinkhole topography is found in many parts of the world, including Florida, Indiana, Missouri, Pennsylvania, and Tennessee in the United States; the Karst region of Serbia; the Salalah region of Arabia; southern China; and many other places where the ground is underlain by limestone.

Sinkholes have many different forms. Some are funnel shaped with boulders and unconsolidated sediment along their bottoms; others are steep-walled pipelike features that have dry or water-filled bottoms. Some sinkholes in southern Oman are up to 900-feet- (274-m-) deep pipes, with caves at their bottoms where residents would get their drinking water until recently, when wells were drilled. Villagers, mostly women, before had to climb down precarious vertical walls and then back out carrying vessels of water. The bottoms of some of these sinkholes are littered with human bones, some dating back thousands of years, of water carriers who slipped on their route. Some of the caves are decorated with prehistoric cave art, showing that these sinkholes were used as water sources for thousands or tens of thousands of years.

Sinkhole formation is intricately linked to the lowering of the water table, as exemplified by Winter Park. When water fills the underground caves and passages, it slowly dissolves the walls, floor, and roof of the chambers, carrying the limestone away in solution. When the water table is lowered by drought, by overpumping of groundwater by people, or by other mechanisms, the roofs of the caves may no longer be supported, and they may catastrophically collapse into the chambers, forming a sinkhole on the surface. In Florida many of the sinkholes formed because officials lowered the water table level to drain parts of the Everglades to make more land available for development. This ill-fated decision was rethought, and attempts have been

A home in Lake City, Florida, on the edge of a sinkhole, March 3, 2005. Lowering of the groundwater table has caused many sinkholes to form in southern Florida in recent years. *(AP)*

made to restore the water table, but in many cases it was too late and the damage was done.

Many sinkholes form suddenly and catastrophically, with the roof of an underground void suddenly collapsing and dropping all of the surface material into the hole. Other sinkholes form more gradually, with the slow movement of loose unconsolidated material into the underground stream network eventually leading to the formation of a surface depression that may continue to grow into a sinkhole.

The pattern of surface subsidence resulting from sinkhole collapse depends on the initial size of the cave that collapses, the depth to the cavity, and the strength of the overlying rock. Big caves that collapse can cause a greater surface effect. For a collapse structure at depth to propagate to the surface, blocks must fall off the roof and into the cavern. The blocks fall by breaking along fractures and falling by the force of gravity. If the overlying material is weak, the fractures will propagate outward, forming a cone-shaped depression with its apex in the original collapse structure. In contrast, if the overlying material is strong, the fractures will propagate vertically upward, resulting in a pipelike collapse structure.

When the roof material collapses into the cavern, blocks of wall rock accumulate on the cavern floor. There is abundant pore space between these blocks so that the collapsed blocks take up a larger volume than they did when they were attached to the walls. In this way the underground collapsed cavern may become completely filled with blocks of the roof and walls before any effect migrates to the surface. If enough pore space is created, then almost no subsidence may occur along the surface. In contrast, if the cavity collapses near the surface, then a collapse pit will eventually form on the surface.

It may take years or decades for a deep collapse structure to migrate from the depth where it initiates to the surface. The first signs of a collapse structure migrating to the surface may be tensional cracks in the soil, bedrock, or building foundations, which are formed as material pulls away from unaffected areas as it subsides. Circular areas of tensional cracks may enclose an area of contractional buckling in the center of the incipient collapse structure, as bending in the center of the collapsing zone forces material together.

After sinkholes form, they may take on several different morphological characteristics. Solution sinkholes are saucer-shaped depressions formed by the dissolution of surface limestone and have a thin cover of soil or loose sediment. These grow slowly and present few hazards, since they are forming on the surface and are not connected to underground stream or collapse structures. Cover-subsidence sinkholes form where the loose surface sediments move slowly downward to fill a growing solution sinkhole. Cover-collapse sinkholes form where a thick section of sediment overlies a large solution cavity at depth, and the cavity is capped by an impermeable layer such as clay or shale. A perched water table develops over the aquiclude. Eventually, the collapse cavity becomes so large that the shale or clay aquiclude unit collapses into the cavern, and the remaining overburden rapidly sinks into the cavern, much like sand sinking in an hourglass. These are some of the most dangerous sinkholes since they form rapidly and may be quite large. Collapse sinkholes are simpler but still dangerous. They form where the strong layers on the surface collapse directly into the cavity, forming steep-walled sinkholes.

Sinkhole topography may continue to mature into a situation in which many of the sinkholes have merged into elongate valleys, and the former surface is found as flat areas on surrounding hills. Even this mature landscape may continue to evolve until tall steep-walled karst towers reach to the former land surface, and a new surface has formed at the level of the former cave floor. The Cantonese region of southern China's Guangxi best shows this type of karst tower terrain.

Detection of Incipient Sinkholes

Some of the damage from sinkhole formation could be avoided if the location and general time of sinkhole formation could be predicted. At present it may be possible to recognize places where sinkholes may be forming by monitoring for the formation of shallow depressions and extensional cracks on the surface, particularly circular depressions. Building foundations can be examined regularly for new cracks, and distances between slabs on bridges with expansion joints can be monitored to check for expansion related to collapse. Other remote sensing and geophysical methods may prove useful for monitoring sinkhole formation, particularly if the formation of a collapse structure is suspected. Shallow seismic waves can detect open spaces, and ground-penetrating radar can be used to map the bedrock surface and to look for collapse structures beneath soils. In some cases it may be worthwhile to drill shallow test holes to determine if there is an open cavity at depth that is propagating toward the surface.

Human-Induced Subsidence

Several types of human activity can result in the formation of sinkholes or cause other surface subsidence phenomena. Withdrawals of fluids from underground aquifers, depletion of the source of replenishment to these aquifers, and collapse of underground mines can all cause surface subsidence. In addition, vibrations from drilling, construction, or blasting can trigger collapse events, and the extra load of buildings over unknown deep collapse structures can cause them to propagate to the surface, forming a sinkhole. These processes reflect geologic hazards caused by human interaction with the natural environment.

MINE COLLAPSE

Mining activities may mimic the formation of natural caves, since mining operations remove material from depth and leave roof materials partly unsupported. There are many examples of mines of different types that have collapsed, resulting in surface subsidence, sinkhole formation, and even the catastrophic draining of large lakes.

The mining of salt has created sinkholes and surface subsidence problems in a number of cases. Salt is mined in several different ways, including the digging of tunnels from which the salt is excavated and by injecting water into a salt deposit, removing the salt-saturated water and drying it to remove the salt for use. This second technique is called solution mining and has less control over where the salt is removed than the classical excavation-style mining. Shallow sinkholes and surface

Ruins of a building in water on Jefferson Island in Lake Peigneur, Louisiana, in 1984. In 1980 the lake was suddenly drained when an oil drill punctured a shaft of a salt-mining tunnel beneath the lake, and the water of the lake drained into the mine. As the mine filled, the lake eventually filled back up, as shown in the photo four years after the disaster. *(CORBIS)*

subsidence are typical and are expected around solution mining operations; for instance, the salt-mining operations near Hutchinson, Kansas, resulted in the formation of dozens of sinkholes, including one nearly 1,000 feet across that partly swallowed the salt processing plant.

One of the most spectacular of all salt-mining subsidence incidents occurred on November 21, 1980, on Lake Peigneur, Louisiana. The center of Lake Peigneur is occupied by a salt dome that forms Jefferson Island. This salt dome was mined extensively with many underground tunnels excavated to remove the salt. Southern Louisiana is also an oil-rich region, and on an ill-fated day in 1980 an oil-drilling rig accidentally drilled a hole into one of the mine shafts. Water began swirling into the hole, and the roof of the mine collapsed, setting the entire lake into a giant spinning whirlpool that quickly drained into the deep mine as if it were bathwater escaping down the drain. The oil-drilling rig, 10 barges, and a tugboat were sucked into the mine shafts, and much of the surrounding land collapsed into the collapse structure, destroying a home and other properties. After the mine was filled with water, the lake gradually filled again, but the damage was done.

Other types of mining have resulted in surface subsidence and collapse, including coal mining in the Appalachians and the Rocky Mountains. Most coal mine–related subsidence occurs where relatively shallow, flat-lying coal seams have been mined, and the mine roofs collapse. The fractures and collapse structures eventually migrate to the surface, leading to elongate trains of sinkholes and other collapse structures.

GROUNDWATER EXTRACTION

The extraction of groundwater, oil, gas, or other fluids from underground reservoirs can cause significant subsidence of the land's surface. In some cases, the removal of underground water is natural. During times of severe drought soil moisture may decrease dramatically, and drought-resistant plants with deep root systems can draw water from great depths, reaching many tens of meters in some cases. In most cases, however, subsidence caused by deep fluid extraction is caused by human activity.

This deep subsidence mechanism operates because the fluids that are extracted help support the weight of the overlying regolith. The weight of the overlying material places the fluids under significant pore pressure, known as hydrostatic pressure, which keeps the pressure between individual grains in the regolith at a minimum. This in turn

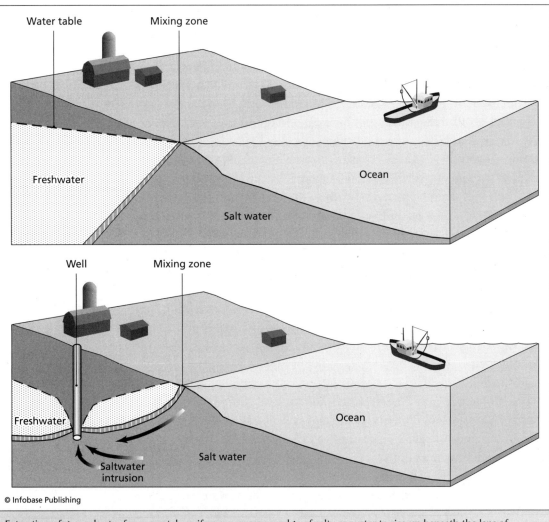

Water table   Mixing zone

Freshwater

Ocean

Salt water

Well   Mixing zone

Freshwater

Ocean

Salt water

Saltwater
intrusion

© Infobase Publishing

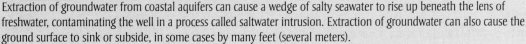

Extraction of groundwater from coastal aquifers can cause a wedge of salty seawater to rise up beneath the lens of freshwater, contaminating the well in a process called saltwater intrusion. Extraction of groundwater can also cause the ground surface to sink or subside, in some cases by many feet (several meters).

helps prevent the grains from becoming closely packed or compacted. If the fluids are removed, the pressure between individual grains increases and the grains become more closely packed and compacted, occupying less space than before the fluid was extracted. This can cause the surface to subside. A small amount of this subsidence may be temporary or recoverable, but generally, once surface subsidence related to fluid extraction occurs, it is nonrecoverable. When this process occurs on the scale of a reservoir or entire basin, the effect can be subsidence of a relatively large area. Subsidence associated with underground fluid extraction is usually gradual but still costs millions of dollars in damage every year in the United States.

The amount of surface subsidence is related to the amount of fluid withdrawn from the ground and also to the compressibility of the layer from which the fluid has been removed. If water is removed from cracks in a solid *igneous,* metamorphic, or sedimentary rock, then the strength of the rock around the cracks will be great enough to support the overlying material, and no surface subsidence is likely to occur. In contrast, if fluids are removed from a compressible layer such as sand, shale, or clay, then significant surface subsidence may result from fluid extraction. Clay and shale have a greater porosity and compressibility than sand, so extraction of water from clay-rich sediments results in greater subsidence than the same amount of fluid withdrawn from a sandy layer.

One of the most common causes of fluid extraction–related subsidence is the overpumping of groundwater from aquifers. If many wells are pumping water from the same aquifer, the cones of depression surrounding each well begin to merge, lowering the regional groundwater level. Lowering of the groundwater table can lead to gradual, irreversible subsidence.

Surface subsidence associated with groundwater extraction is a serious problem in many parts of the southwestern United States. Many cities such as Tucson, Phoenix, Los Angeles, Salt Lake City, Las Vegas, and San Diego rely heavily on groundwater pumped from compressible layers in underground aquifers.

The San Joaquin Valley of California offers a dramatic example of the effects of groundwater extraction. Extraction of groundwater for irrigation over a period of 50 years has resulted in nearly 30 feet of surface subsidence. Parts of the Tucson Basin in Arizona are presently subsiding at an accelerating rate, and many investigators fear that the increasing rate of subsidence reflects a transition from temporary recoverable subsidence to a permanent compaction of the water-bearing layers at depth.

The world's most famous subsiding city is Venice, Italy. Venice is sinking at a rate of about one foot per century, and much of the city is below sea level or just above sea level and is prone to floods from storm surges and astronomical high tides in the Adriatic Sea. These *aqua altas* ("high waters" in Italian) flood streets as far as the famous Piazza San Marco. The city has subsided more than 10 feet (3 m) since it was founded near sea level. Venice has been subsiding for a combination of

Dog and fire hydrant in Long Beach, California, 1950s, showing subsidence. The land surface used to be at the height of the base of the hydrant at the top of the long pipe, but extraction of fluids (water and oil) from beneath the surface caused the land surface to sink, placing the hydrant out of reach. *(LBGO)*

reasons, including compaction of the coastal muds that the city was built on. One of the main causes of the sinking of Venice has been groundwater extraction. Nearly 20,000 groundwater wells pumped water from compressible sediment beneath the city, with the result being that the city sank into the empty space created by the withdrawal of water. The Italian government has now built an aqueduct system to bring drinking water to residents and has closed most of its 20,000 wells. This action has slowed the subsidence of the city, but it is still sinking, and this action may be too little, too late to spare Venice from the future effects of storm surges and astronomical high tides.

Mexico City is also plagued with subsidence problems caused by groundwater extraction. Mexico City is built on a several-thousand-foot- (~1,000-m) thick sequence of sedimentary and volcanic rocks, as well as a large, dried lake bed on the surface. Most of the groundwater is extracted from the upper 200 feet (61 m) of these sediments. Parts of Mexico City have subsided dramatically, whereas others have not. The northeast part of the city has subsided about 20 feet (6 m). Many of the subsidence patterns in Mexico City can be related to the underlying geology. In places such as the northeast part of the city that are underlain by loose compressible sediments, the subsidence has been large. In places underlain by volcanic rocks, the subsidence has been minor.

The extraction of oil, natural gas, and other fluids from the earth also may result in surface subsidence. In the United States subsidence related to petroleum extraction is a large problem in Texas, Louisiana, and parts of California. One of the worst cases of oil field subsidence is that of Long Beach, California, where the ground surface has subsided 30 feet (9 m) in response to extraction of underground oil. There are approximately 2,000 oil wells in Long Beach, pumping oil from beneath the city. Much of Long Beach's coastal area subsided below sea level, forcing the city to construct a series of dikes to keep the water out. When the subsidence problem was recognized and understood, the city began a program of reinjecting water into the oil field to replace the extracted fluids and to prevent further subsidence. This reinjection program was initiated in 1958, and since then the subsidence has stopped, but the land surface can not be pumped up again to its former levels.

Pumping of oil from an oil field west of Marina del Rey in Los Angeles, along the Newport-Inglewood Fault, resulted in subsidence beneath the Baldwin Hills Dam and Reservoir and the dam's catastrophic failure on December 14, 1963. Oil extraction from the Inglewood oil field resulted in subsidence-related slip on a fault beneath the dam and reservoir, which was enough to initiate a crack in the dam's foundation. The crack was quickly expanded by pressure from the water in the reservoir. At 3:38 P.M. 65 million gallons of water were suddenly released, destroying dozens of homes, killing five people, and causing $12 million in damage.

Subsidence Caused by Drought and Surface Water Overuse

Drought and overuse of surface water can also lead to subsidence by depriving the groundwater system of the water that would normally replenish the aquifer. If the drought or overuse of the surface water persists for years, then the sediments in the aquifer may begin to compact, leading to surface subsidence. One of the more dramatic examples of the effects of surface water use leading to subsidence is provided by the water problem along the Jordan River on the Israeli-Jordanian border. Water in the Jordan is needed by the thirsty population in this dry area, and the greatly decreased flow of the Jordan caused by this water use has caused subsidence of the Dead Sea by about 1.5–2 inches (0.5–1 cm) per year. This subsidence caused by lack of groundwater replenishment is in addition to the tectonic subsidence in the Dead Sea pull-apart basin. The total subsidence is now about 20 feet (6 m) since 1998, putting the Dead Sea at a startling 1,400 feet (427 m) below sea level.

Subsidence from Earthquake Ground Displacements

Sometimes individual large earthquakes may displace the land surface vertically, resulting in subsidence or uplift. One of the largest and best-documented cases of earthquake-induced subsidence resulted from a magnitude 9.2 earthquake in southern Alaska on March 27, 1964. This earthquake tilted a huge—approximately 77,000 square mile (200,000 km²)—area of the Earth's crust. Significant changes in ground level were recorded along the coast for more than 620 miles (1,000 km), including uplifts of up to 36 feet (11 m), subsidence of up to 6.5 feet (2 m), and lateral shifts of 10–40 feet (3–10 m). Much of the area that subsided was along Cook Inlet north to Anchorage, Valdez, and south to Kodiak Island. Towns that were built around docks prior to the earthquake were suddenly located below the high tide mark, and entire towns had to move to higher ground. F orests that subsided found their root systems suddenly inundated by salt water, leading to the death of the forests. Populated areas located at previously safe distances from the high tide (and storm) line became prone to flooding and storm surges and had to be relocated.

TECTONIC SUBSIDENCE

The slow movement of tectonic plates on the Earth's surface is associated with subsidence of many types and scales, particularly on or near plate boundaries. In many cases it is difficult to separate the effects of tectonic subsidence from subsidence caused by groundwater extraction, compaction, and other causes. Plate tectonics is associated with the large-scale vertical motions that uplift entire mountain ranges, drop basins to lower elevations, and form elongate half-mile-deep depressions in the Earth's surface known as rifts. Plate tectonics also causes the broad flat coastal plains and *passive margins* to slowly subside relative to sea level, moving the sea slowly into the continents. More local-scale folding and faulting can cause areas of the land surface to rise or sink, although at rates that rarely exceed 0.39 inch (1 cm) per year. Plate tectonics also ultimately causes the deposition of sedimentary layers that serve as aquifers and tilts these layers during movement of the plates, driving groundwater and surface water movements from high elevations to low elevations.

Extensional plate boundaries are naturally associated with subsidence, since these boundaries occur in places where the crust is being pulled apart, thinning, and sinking relative to sea level. Places where the continental crust has ruptured and is extending are known as continental rifts. In the United States the Rio Grande rift in New Mexico represents a place where the crust has begun to rupture, and it is subsiding relative to surrounding mountain ranges. In this area the actual subsidence does not present much of a hazard, as the land is not near the sea, and a large region is subsiding. The net effect is that the valley floor is slightly lower in elevation every year than it was the year before. The rifting and subsidence is sometimes associated with faulting when the basin floor suddenly drops,

(continues)

(continued)

and the *earthquakes* are associated with their own sets of hazards. Rifting in the Rio Grande is also associated with the rise of a large body of magma beneath Soccoro, and if this magma body has an eruption, it is likely to be catastrophic.

Large areas of the Basin and Range Province of the southwestern United States are also subsiding. The region was topographically uplifted millions of years ago, and tectonic stresses are now pulling the entire region apart, causing locally rapid subsidence in the basins between ranges. Again the main hazards from this type of subsidence are mainly associated with the earthquakes that sometimes accommodate the extension and subsidence.

The world's most extensive continental rift province is found in East Africa. An elongate subsiding rift depression extends from Ethiopia and Somalia in the north and south through Kenya, Uganda, Rwanda, Burundi, and Tanzania, then swings back toward the coast through Malawi and Mozambique. The East African rift system contains the oldest hominid fossils and is also host to areas of rapid land surface subsidence. Earthquakes are common, as are volcanic eruptions, such as the catastrophic eruption of Nyiragongo, Democratic Republic of the Congo, in January 2002. *Lava* flows from Nyiragongo covered large parts of the town of Goma, forcing residents to flee to neighboring Rwanda.

Subsidence in the East African rift system has formed a series of very deep, elongate lakes, including Lakes Edward, Albert, Kivu, Malawi, and Tanganyika. These lakes sit on narrow basin floors that are bounded on their east and west sides by steep rift escarpments. The shoulders of the rifts slope away from the center of the rift, so sediments carried by streams do not enter the rift but are carried away from it. This allows the rift lakes to become very deep without being filled by sediments. It also means that additional subsidence can cause parts of the rift floor to subside well below sea level, such as at Lake Abe in the Awash depression in the Afar rift. This lake and several other areas near Djibouti rest hundreds of feet below sea level. These lakes, by virtue of being so deep, become stratified with respect to dissolved oxygen, methane, and other gases. Methane is locally extracted from these lakes for fuel, although periodic overturning of the lakes' waters can lead to hazardous release of gases.

Transform plate boundaries, where one plate slides past another, can also be sites of hazardous subsidence. The strike-slip faults that make up transform plate boundaries are rarely perfectly straight. Places where the faults bend may be sites of uplift of mountains or rapid subsidence of narrow elongate basins. The orientation of the bend in the fault system determines whether the bend is associated with contraction and the formation of mountains, or extension, subsidence, and the formation of the elongate basins known as pull-apart basins. Pull-apart basins typically subside quickly, have steep escarpments marked by active faults on at least two sides, and may have volcanic activity. Some of the topographically lowest places on Earth are in pull-apart basins, including the Salton Sea in California and the Dead Sea along the border between Israel and Jordan. The hazards in pull-apart basins are very much like those in continental rifts.

Convergent plate boundaries are known for tectonic uplift, although they may also be associated with regional subsidence. When a mountain range is pushed along a fault on top of a plate boundary, the underlying plate may subside rapidly. In most situations erosion of the overriding mountain range sheds enormous amounts of loose sediment onto the underriding plate, so the land surface does not actually subside, although any particular rock layer will be buried and subside rapidly.

Compaction-Related Subsidence on Deltas and Passive Margin Coastal Areas

Subsidence related to compaction and removal of water from sediments deposited on continental margin deltas, in lake beds, and in other wetlands poses a serious problem to residents trying to cope with the hazards of life at sea level. Deltas are especially prone to subsidence, because the sediments that are deposited on deltas are very water rich, and the weight of overlying new sediments compacts existing material, forcing the water out of pore spaces. Deltas are also constructed along continental shelves that are prone to regional-scale tectonic subsidence and are subject to additional subsidence forced by the weight of the sedimentary burden deposited on the entire margin. Continental margin deltas are rarely more than a few feet above sea level, so they are prone to the effects of tides, storm surges, river floods, and other coastal disasters, as demonstrated in 2005 by Hurricanes Katrina and Rita along the Mississippi River Delta, and by Cyclone Sidr that struck the delta of Bangladesh in November 2007. Any decrease in the sediment supply to keep the land in these areas at sea level has serious ramifications, subjecting the area to subsidence below sea level.

Some of the world's thickest sedimentary deposits are formed in deltas on the continental shelves, and these are of considerable economic importance because they also host the world's largest petroleum reserves. The continental shelves are divided into many different sedimentary environments. Beaches contain the coarse fraction of material deposited at the ocean front by rivers and sea cliff erosion. Quartz is typically very abundant, because of its resistance to weathering and its abundance in the crust. Beach sands tend to be well-rounded, as is any other beach material, such as beach glass, because of the continuous abrasion caused by the waves dragging the particles back and forth. Many of the sediments transported by rivers are deposited in estuaries, which are semi-enclosed bodies of water near the coast in which freshwater and seawater mix. Near-shore sediments deposited in estuaries include thick layers of mud, sand, and silt. Many estuaries are slowly subsiding and become filled with thick sedimentary deposits. Deltas are formed where streams and rivers meet the ocean, and they drop their loads because of the reduced flow velocity. Deltas are complex sedimentary systems with coarse stream channels, fine-grained interchannel sediments, and a gradation seaward to deep water deposits of silt and mud.

All the sediments deposited in the coastal environments tend to be water rich when deposited and thus subject to water loss and compaction. Subsidence poses the greatest hazard on deltas, because these sediments tend to be the thickest of all those deposited on continental shelves. They are typically fine-grained muds and shales that suffer the greatest water loss and compaction. Unfortunately, deltas are also the sites of some of the world's largest cities, since they offer great river ports. New Orleans, Shanghai, and many other major cities have been built on delta deposits and have subsided several meters since they were first built. Many other cities built on these very compactible shelf sediments are also experiencing dangerous amounts of subsidence.

There are major consequences of this subsidence for people who live in these cities. Many uncertainties remain about how they will be affected by increased rates of subsidence relative to sea level caused by damming rivers that trap replenishing sediments upstream. These cities need to appraise how to deal with current sea level rise, estimated to be occurring at a rate of an inch (2.5 cm) every 10 years with more than six inches (15 cm) of rise in the past century. Whatever the response, it

Two firefighters work beside a bus stuck in a hole in Shanghai, China, September 28, 2004. Water flooded a street and nearby houses after an underground water pipe exploded due to gradual ground subsidence. *(AP)*

will be costly. Some urban and government planners estimate that protecting the populace from sea level rise on subsiding coasts will be the costliest endeavor ever undertaken by humans.

The natural subsidence in these coastal delta cities has been accelerated by human activities. The construction of tall heavy buildings on loose, compactible, water-rich sediments forces water out of the pore spaces of the sediment underlying each building, causing that building to subside. The weight of cities also has a cumulative effect, and big cities built on deltas and other compactible sediment cause a regional flow of water out of underlying sediments, leading to subsidence of the city as a whole.

New Orleans has one of the worst subsidence problems of coastal cities in the United States. Its rate and total amount of subsidence are not the highest, but since nearly half of the city is at or below sea level, any additional subsidence will put the city dangerously far below sea level. Already the Mississippi River is higher than downtown streets, and ships float by at the second-story level of buildings. Levees keep the river at bay and in some cases keep storm surges from inundating the city. Additional subsidence will make these measures impractical. New Orleans, Houston, and other coastal cities have been accelerating their own sinking by withdrawing groundwater and oil from compactible sediments beneath the cities, although much of this has been halted in recent years, when officials recognized that they were literally pulling the ground out from under their own feet.

The combined effects of natural and human-induced subsidence, plus the global sea level rise, have resulted in increased urban flooding of many cities and greater destruction during storms. Storm barriers have been built in some cases, but this is only the beginning. Thousands of miles of barriers will need to be built to protect these cities unless billions of people are willing to relocate to inland areas, which is an unlikely prospect.

There are several steps that can be taken to reduce the risks from coastal subsidence. First, a more intelligent regulation of groundwater extraction from coastal aquifers and of oil from coastal regions must be enforced. If oil is pumped out of an oil reservoir, then water should be pumped back in to prevent subsidence. Sea level is rising partly from natural astronomical effects and partly from human-induced changes to the atmosphere. It is not too early to start planning for sea level rises of a few feet. Sea walls should be designed and tested before construction on massive scales. Businesses and individuals should consider moving many operations inland to higher ground.

Mitigation of Property Damage from Subsidence and Compaction

Most of the hazards and damage from subsidence, compaction, and collapse is to buildings constructed on material that is differentially sinking. Buildings are forced to either accommodate the changing volume of their foundations or to crack and crumble.

The most severe compaction is on soils and regolith made of organic and clay-rich soils, such as those on deltas, wetlands, and in artificially filled areas including reclaimed landfills. As building sites become scarce, it is becoming increasingly common to fill in marshes and wetlands and to reclaim old landfills for construction sites. When buildings are constructed on the organic-rich, clay-rich, poorly compacted soils, the weight of the artificial fill and the buildings may be enough to force water out of the underlying pore spaces, causing compaction and subsidence. The hazards from this type of compaction are most severe if parts of the surface compact and subside more than other nearby parts. This differential subsidence can result from uneven thickness of the compacting layer or from buildings that have unequal weights in different parts of the structure, exerting different stresses on underlying soils and thus causing differential compaction. Differential subsidence causes cracks in foundations and walls, causes pipelines and plumbing systems to be disrupted, and it can disrupt the regular flow of groundwater by changing the local slopes of underground units.

Conducting geological surveys before construction and adhering to proper construction techniques can reduce some of the damage from compaction and subsidence. All structures built on compactible regolith should be supported by pilings driven through the compressible layer to a noncompressible, competent layer such as bedrock, sand, or gravel. Pipelines should be constructed with flexible joints to accommodate differential compaction, and bridges should have expansion joints to accommodate differential movement between support pillars.

Some types of soils and regolith have proven particularly prone to compaction and subsidence, and even more stringent measures are needed to mitigate hazards of construction. *Shrink-swell* clays are notorious for compacting in dry seasons, causing millions of dollars of damage to foundations, bridges, and pipelines. In many cases the best solution is to totally remove the shrink-swell clay from the site and replace it with suitably compacted nonswelling material, such as sand and gravel. This technique is especially expensive and is not often done. In most cases reinforcing concrete with extra rebarb (steel rods) so that foundations and walls do not pull apart as the clay dries and shrinks mitigates the hazard, and buildings are placed on deep pilings that extend past the *expansive clay.*

Organic-rich soils are also particularly hazardous because of their enormous compaction potential. Organic-rich soils are formed in wetlands such as swamps and are common in coastal marshes and deltas. These organic-rich soils are very water rich when they accumulate, and when the wetland or region containing the soil is drained, the soil compacts and air enters the pore spaces and begins to oxidize the organic material into soil. This oxidation results in the decomposition of the organic material, and decomposed organic matter occupies less space than the original material, resulting in compaction of the soil. This type of compaction of organic-rich soil is a major problem in old lake beds, deltas, wetlands, and coastal wetlands.

Buildings constructed on organic-rich soils should be built on pilings that extend below the organic-rich layer, if possible. On deltas this is not generally possible since the organic-rich layers may extend for several miles below the surface. Homes and businesses built on pilings on reclaimed wetlands and coastal marshes often appear to be emerging, or rising, every year out of the ground on long concrete pilings. The ground is really sinking faster than the buildings, creating this illusion. Continued compaction and subsidence of the organic-rich soils may cause the buildings to collapse off their pilings. New material should be regularly added beneath these structures to prevent them from toppling off unsupported pilings.

Conclusion

Natural subsidence has many causes and inflicts huge financial losses, even though the process of subsidence is usually imperceptibly slow. Dissolution of limestone by underground streams and water systems is one of the most common, creating large open spaces that collapse under the influence of gravity. Groundwater dissolution results in the formation of sinkholes, which are large, generally circular depressions that are caused by collapse of the surface into underground open spaces.

Subsidence can also have tectonic driving mechanisms. Earthquakes may raise or lower the land suddenly, as in the case of the 1964 Alaskan earthquake, when tens of thousands of square miles suddenly sank or rose three to five feet (1–1.5 m), causing massive disruption to coastal communities and ecosystems. Earthquake-induced ground shaking can also cause *liquefaction* and compaction of unconsolidated surface sediments, also leading to subsidence. Regional lowering of the land surface by liquefaction and compaction is known from the massive 1811 and 1812 earthquakes in New Madrid, Missouri, and from many other examples.

Volcanic activity can cause subsidence, as when underground magma chambers empty out during an eruption. In this case subsidence is often the lesser of many hazards that local residents need to fear. Subsidence may also occur on lava flows when lava empties out of tubes or underground chambers.

Some natural subsidence on the regional scale is associated with continental scale tectonic processes. The weight of sediments deposited along continental shelves can cause the entire continental margin to sink, causing coastal subsidence and a landward migration of the shoreline. Tectonic processes associated with extension, continental rifting, strike-slip faulting, and even collision can cause local or regional subsidence, sometimes at rates of several inches (> 5 cm) per year.

7

Summary

Water is the most precious resource in the world, needed for all life functions and serving as a transportation medium, for irrigation and watering animals, and for drinking. Of all water on the planet 97 percent is salty, and only a quarter of the remaining 3 percent is available for human use. In many parts of the world water resources are stretched to the limit, and people are dying of thirst or drinking severely contaminated water and getting diseases from it. In other parts of the world water is present in excess, and massive floods cover cities and regions. With an exponentially growing world population, governments need to assess how the water supply will respond to a changing climate and do so accordingly. Many regions will need to begin expensive desalination or find other groundwater resources to feed their populations.

Freshwater on the land surface flows in streams and rivers, which are dynamic systems that change their channel patterns and positions in response to changes in the amount of water in the system, the slope, the amount of sediments carried, and the ease at which material is entrained from the banks into the stream. Different channel patterns, such as straight, meandering, and braided, represent delicate balances between these variables and the forces that drive and resist streamflow. Rivers naturally migrate back and forth across their floodplains, which are an integral part of river systems. Any attempts to alter the systems, such as constricting the river into a narrow channel and forbidding it from migrating laterally, will result in changes to other parts of the system. When levees constrict a river, the base tends to rise, necessitating further heightening of levees.

Eventually levees collapse, initiating disasters, such as the two levee failures along the Yellow River in China in the past 150 years, each of which caused a million fatalities. Urbanization of the floodplain also has important consequences for river dynamics. Paving over the floodplain not only destroys this critical ecosystem but also causes water to flow quickly across the surface instead of being stored in the porous sediments. The resulting floods rise faster, reach greater heights, have higher velocities and are more erosive, and dissipate faster than the natural, slowly rising, fertilizing floods that the river would naturally deliver.

Many rivers of the world have been confined by levees, in attempts to control floods and improve navigation. The Mississippi River and many of its tributaries have been nearly completely channelized since levees were first constructed when Europeans arrived in New Orleans in the early 1700s. There is a long history of building levees, seeing the floodwaters rise higher than before, building the levees higher, then experiencing higher floods. It was not until the 1970s that scientists were able to quantitatively show that building levees and confining the rivers make floods worse. Despite this, levees continue to be built, and politicians and developers reassure unsuspecting residents that the levees are safe and will protect them from floods.

Floods may occur in most parts of the world, from coastal plains to the Tropics, arctic, and desert, and even in mountainous environments. Floods are a stream or river system's natural response to above-normal amounts of rainfall, snowmelts, or storms. Small streams respond to high amounts of rainfall by overflowing their banks quickly, whereas large rivers rise and recede more slowly, generally in response to above-average rainfalls in a large drainage basin for an extended period of time. Such long-term regional floods have caused some of the highest death tolls from any natural hazard. Floods have also caused rivers to change course, wreaking havoc on transportation routes, urban and agricultural land use, and drastic changes to natural ecosystems. Some floods have covered regions with water for months; other floods have killed millions of people. Other places in the world are experiencing severe drought or see rapidly expanding populations in regions that do not receive large rainfalls, so these regions have had to import water from far away in aqueduct systems. In other places, particularly the Middle East, the water shortage is at such a critical level in a region plagued with strife that it is likely that a war over water will be fought in the near future.

There is 35 times as much water beneath the land in the groundwater system than in all the lakes, streams, and rivers combined. This water moves slowly and can be used wisely for drinking water and irrigation, but groundwater must be treated as a slowly renewable mineral resource, since many regions are using it faster than it is being replenished by infiltration from rain and snowmelt. There are many examples where groundwater aquifers have been contaminated by chemicals leaking from gas stations, toxic waste dumps, septic systems, or road salts. There are horrific examples of people becoming seriously diseased and dying from contaminants in the groundwater. Greater care must be taken to preserve the quality of water in underground aquifers.

Extraction of groundwater has led to significant subsidence of the land surface in places such as coastal California, Las Vegas, Long Island, New York, and many locations around the world. This problem is most severe when the groundwater is extracted from a coastal aquifer, and seawater moves in under the freshwater table to replace the lost freshwater. This process is known as seawater incursion and contaminates aquifers and wells with salt water, making them useless.

Subsidence has other causes than just extraction of groundwater. Karst terrains are found around the world and represent places where groundwater has dissolved rocks such as limestone, typically opening up small fractures into larger caverns. When the groundwater table is lowered, the caves are opened and either exposed at the surface or exist as open caverns at depth. In Florida the groundwater table was lowered to make more land available for development, but the consequence was that many sinkholes opened up, swallowing homes, cars, and roads. The surface can also subside when water is forced out of the pore space of clay, sand, and organic soils as they are compacted under the weight of additional sediments on deltas or as the organic matter decays. This compaction, plus regional tectonic subsidence, and sea level rise combine to make serious problems for coastal cities built on deltas, such as New Orleans. Some of these places are already far below sea level and sinking at rates of up to an inch or more per year, so in the next century some of these sites may be located far offshore from the landward-moving coastline.

Politicians, planners, and scientists need to come to terms with a limited water supply in a growing world and the implications of climate change on these systems. Floods, droughts, rising sea levels, and changing climate are all interacting with a growing world population, and better understanding of scientific problems will help people move out of harm's way, best using the planet's water resources.

Glossary

aggradation—Deposition of sediments along a riverbed that causes the bed to rise

antecedent stream—A stream that has maintained its course across topography that is being uplifted by tectonic forces; these streams cross high ridges

anthropogenic—Caused by humans

aquiclude—A rock or soil unit that stops the movement of water

aquifer—Any body of permeable rock or regolith saturated with water through which groundwater moves

aquitard—A rock or soil unit that restricts the flow of water

artesian pressure, spring, system—A permeable layer, typically a sandstone, that is confined between two impermeable beds, creating a confined aquifer. In these systems water only enters the system in a small recharge area, and if this is in the mountains, then the aquifer may be under considerable pressure. This is known as an artesian system.

avulsion—The process in which a river breaks through a river levee and flows onto the floodplain

bed load—The coarse particles that move along or close to the bottom of the streambed

braid bar—A gravel and sand bar that separates one of the interconnected channels in a braided stream

capacity—The potential load a stream can carry, measured in the amount (volume) of sediment passing a given point in a set amount of time

cavitation—A process that occurs when a stream's velocity is so high that the vapor pressure of water is exceeded and bubbles begin to form on rigid surfaces. These bubbles alternately form and then collapse with tremendous pressure, and form an extremely effective erosive agent.

chemical weathering—Decomposition of rocks through the alteration of individual mineral grains

climate—The average weather of a place or region

climate change—The phenomena whereby global temperatures, patterns of precipitation, wind, and ocean currents change in response to human and natural causes

coastal plain—A relatively flat area along the coast that was formerly below sea level during past high sea level

compaction—A phenomenon in which the pore spaces of a material are gradually reduced, condensing the material by expelling the water between the grains, and causing the surface to subside

competence—The maximum size of particles that can be entrained and transported by a stream under a given set of hydraulic conditions, measured in diameter of largest bed load

consequent stream—A stream whose course is determined by the direction of the slope of the land

convergent plate boundary—A place where two plates move toward each other, resulting in one plate sliding beneath the other when a dense oceanic plate is involved or collision and deformation when continental plates are involved. These types of plate boundaries may have the largest of all earthquakes.

cyclone—A tropical storm equivalent to a hurricane that forms in the Indian Ocean

delta—A low, flat deposit of alluvium at the mouth of a stream or river that forms a broad triangular or irregular-shaped area that extends into a bay, ocean, or lake. Deltas are typically crossed by many distributaries from the main river and may extend for a considerable distance underwater.

dendritic drainage—A randomly branching pattern that forms on horizontal strata or on rocks with uniform erosional resistance

desalination—Any number of individual processes that remove salt from water and make it potable, or fit for drinking

discharge—Amount of water moving past a point in a stream, usually measured in cubic feet or cubic meters per second

discharge area—Area where water leaves the groundwater system

dissolved load—Dissolved chemicals, such as bicarbonate, calcium, sulfate, chloride, sodium, magnesium, and potassium. The dissolved load tends to be high in streams fed by groundwater.

drainage basin—The total area that contributes water to a stream. The line that divides different drainage basins is known as a divide.

drought—A period when the yearly rainfall for a region is significantly less than normal

earthquake—A sudden release of energy from slip on a fault, an explosion, or other event that causes the ground to shake and vibrate, associated with passage of waves of energy released at its source. An earthquake originates in one place and then spreads out in all directions along the fault plane.

ecosystem—A collection of the organisms and surrounding physical elements that together are unique to a specific environment

entrainment—The picking up of particles from the bed load of a stream and the erosion of material from the banks

expansive clay and soil—A soil that adds layers of water molecules between the plates of clay minerals (made of silica, aluminum, and oxygen), loosely bonding the water in the mineral and that is capable of expanding by up to 50 percent more than its dry volume

extensional plate boundary—An extensional or divergent boundary or margin where two plates move apart, creating a void that is typically filled by new oceanic crust that wells up to fill the opening hole

flash floods—A flood that rises suddenly, typically as a wall of water in a narrow canyon

flood—Abnormally high water, typically when a river flows out of its banks

floodplain—A flat area adjacent to a river that naturally floods and generally consists of unconsolidated sediments deposited by the river

fracture zone aquifer—Many buried granite and other bedrock bodies are cut by many fractures, faults, and other cracks, some of which may have open spaces along them. Fractures at various scales represent zones of increased porosity and permeability. They may form networks and therefore are able to store and carry vast amounts of water.

global warming—A trend in climate where the global average yearly temperature is progressively warmer over many years

graded stream—A stream that has gradually adjusted its gradient to reach an equilibrium between sedimentary load, slope, and discharge

gradient—A measure of the vertical drop over a given horizontal distance

granite, granodiorite—Common igneous rock types in the continental crust. The density of granodiorite is 2.6 g/cm^3; its mineralogy includes quartz, plagioclase, biotite, and some potassium feldspar. Granite has more quartz than granodiorite. The volcanic or extrusive equivalent of granite is rhyolite, and of granodiorite, andesite.

greenhouse gas—A gas such as CO_2 that when built up in the atmosphere tends to keep solar heat in the atmosphere, resulting in global warming

groundwater—All the water contained within spaces in bedrock, soil, and regolith

heat capacity—A measure of how much energy can be absorbed by a body without changing its temperature

heat of vaporization—Amount of energy to change water from a liquid state to a vapor

hurricane—A tropical cyclone in which an organized group of thunderstorms rotate about a central low pressure center and have a sustained wind speed of 74 MPH (118 kph)

hydraulic gradient—The pressure difference between the elevation of the source area and the discharge area

hydraulic piping—Where water finds a weak passage through a levee

hydrologic, or water, cycle—Changes, both long and short term, in the Earth's hydrosphere

hydrosphere—A dynamic mass of liquid, continuously on the move between the different reservoirs on land and in the oceans and atmosphere. The hydrosphere includes all the water in oceans, lakes, streams, glaciers, atmosphere, and groundwater, although most water is in the oceans.

igneous rock—A rock that has crystallized from a molten state known as magma. These rocks include plutonic rocks, crystallized below the surface, and volcanic rocks, that have crystallized at the surface.

karst terrain—An area that is affected by groundwater dissolution, cave complexes, and sinkhole development

laminar flow—In a stream, where paths of water particles are parallel and smooth, and the flow is not very erosive. Resistance to flow in laminar systems is provided by internal friction between individual water molecules, and the resistance is proportional to flow velocity.

lava—Magma, or molten rock, that flows at the surface of the Earth

levee—A mound of dirt, clay, or other material that is built along the banks of a river or lake. Levees may be natural or enhanced by people.

liquefaction—A process where sudden shaking of certain types of water-saturated sands and muds turns these once-solid sediments into a slurry, a substance with a liquid-like consistency. Liquefaction occurs when individual grains move apart, and then water moves up in between the individual grains making the whole water-sediment mixture behave like a fluid.

mass wasting—The movement of material downhill without the direct involvement of water

meander—A gentle bend in the trace of a river

molecular attraction—The force that makes thin films of water stick to things, instead of being forced to the ground by gravity

mudflow—A downslope flow that resembles a debris flow, except it has a higher concentration of water (up to 30 percent), which makes it more fluid, with a consistency ranging from soup to wet concrete. Mudflows often start as a muddy stream in a dry mountain canyon, which as it moves picks up more and more mud and sand, until eventually the front of the stream is a wall of moving mud and rock

orographic effect—The process where clouds move over a mountain range and cool, they can hold less water so drop this as precipitation on the windward side of the range. As the air mass moves down the leeward side of the mountain, it warms and is able to hold more moisture than is present, so the leeward sides of mountains tend to be dry.

overland flow—The movement of runoff in broad sheets

oxbow lake—An elongate and curved lake formed by an abandoned meandering stream channel on a floodplain

passive margin—A boundary between continental and oceanic crust that is not a plate boundary, characterized by thick deposits of sedimentary rocks. These margins typically have a flat shallow water shelf, then a steep dropoff to deep oceanfloor rocks away from the continent

perched water table—Domed pockets of water at elevations higher than the main water table, resting on top of the impermeable layer

permeability—A body's capacity to transmit fluids or to allow the fluids to move through its open pore spaces

plate tectonics—A model that describes the process related to the slow motions of more than a dozen rigid plates of solid rock on the surface of the Earth. The plates ride on a deeper layer of partially molten material that is found at depths starting at 60 to 200 miles (100–320 km) beneath the surface of the continents and 1–100 miles (1–160 km) beneath the oceans.

point bar—Deposits of sand and gravel along the inner bends of meandering streams

pore pressure—In piles of sediments, the weight of the overlying material places the fluids under significant pore pressure, known as hydrostatic pressure, which keeps the pressure between individual grains in the regolith at a minimum. This in turn helps prevent the grains from becoming closely packed or compacted.

porosity—The percentage of the total volume of a body that consists of open spaces

recharge area—An area where water enters the groundwater system

recurrence interval—Time interval between floods of a specific discharge

regolith—The outer surface layer of the Earth, consisting of a mixture of soil, organic material, and partially weathered bedrock

residence time—Average length of time that a substance remains in the groundwater system

runoff—Water that falls as rain or snow and flows across the surface into streams or rivers instead of being absorbed into the groundwater system

saltation—The movement of a particle by short intermittent jumps caused by the current's lifting the particles

sapping—The seeping of groundwater that moves along the gravel and sand layers out along the riverbank. This movement of groundwater can carry sediment away from the bank into the stream.

shrink-swell potential—In soil, a measure of a soil's ability to add or lose water at a molecular level

sinkhole—A large, generally circular depression that is caused by collapse of the surface into underground open spaces

sinuosity—The ratio of the stream length to valley length

slide—In mass wasting when rock, soil, water, and debris move over and in contact with the underlying surface

slump—A type of mass wasting where a large mass of rock or sediment moves downward and outward along an upward curving fault surface. Slumps may occur undersea or on the land surface.

spring—Place where groundwater flows out at the ground surface

stalagmite—Cave formation that is pipelike in structure and grows up from the floor of caves, formed by accumulation of calcium carbonate from dripping water

stalagtite—Cave formation that is pipelike in structure and hangs from the roof of a cave, formed by dripping water, typically composed of calcium carbonate

storm surge—An unusually high elevation of water that is formed by water that is pushed ahead of storms and typically moves on land as exceptionally high tide in front of severe ocean storms

stream capture—An event when headland erosion diverts one stream and its drainage into another drainage basin

stream flow—The flow of surface water in well-defined channels

subsequent stream—A stream whose course has become adjusted so that it occupies a belt of weak rock or another geologic structure

subsidence—The sinking of one surface, such as the land, relative to another surface, such as sea level

superposed stream—A stream whose course was laid down in overlying strata onto unlike strata below

suspended load—The fine particles suspended in the stream. These make many streams muddy, and it consists of silt and clay that moves at the same or slightly lower velocity as the stream

terrace—A flat area sitting above the present floodplain level that is an abandoned floodplain formed when a stream flowed above its present channel and floodplain level

thalweg—A line connecting the deepest parts of the channel

transform plate boundary—Place where two plates slide past each other, such as along the San Andreas Fault in California, and often has large earthquakes known as transform boundaries

transmissivity—The ability of a substance to allow water to move through it

transpiration—The evaporation of water from the exposed parts of plants

trellis drainage—Parallel, main stream channels intersected at nearly right angles by tributaries

turbulent flow—In a flowing stream, where water may move in different directions and often forms zones of sideways or short backward flows called eddies. These significantly increase the resistance to flow. In turbulent flows the resistance is proportional to the square of the flow velocity.

urbanization—The process of building up and populating a natural habitat or environment such that the habitat or environment no longer responds to input the way it did before being altered by humans

wadi—A dry streambed. This term is commonly used in Arabic countries.

water resources—Any sources of water that are potentially available for human use, including lakes, rivers, rainfall, reservoirs, and the groundwater system

water table—The boundary between the saturated and unsaturated zones

Further Reading and Web Sites

BOOKS

Barras, J., S. Beville, D. Britsch, et al. *Historical and Projected Coastal Louisiana Land Changes: 1978–2050.* USGS Open File Report OFR 03-334, 2050. Reston, Va.: U.S. Geological Survey. This government-issued book reports the results of an in-depth analysis of how much land has been and will be lost in southern Louisiana due to coastal subsidence and sea level rise.

Beck, B. F. *Engineering and Environmental Implications of Sinkholes and Karst.* Rotterdam, Netherlands: Balkema, 1989. This is an advanced book on how to reduce the damage from sinkholes.

Botkin, D., and E. Keller. *Environmental Science.* Hoboken, N.J.: John Wiley & Sons, 2003. This is an introductory college-level book that discusses many issues of environmental sciences.

Bryant, E. A. *Natural Hazards.* Cambridge: Cambridge University Press, 1991. This is a moderately advanced textbook on the science of natural hazards.

Buros, O. K. *The ABCs of Desalting.* Topsfield, Mass.: International Desalination Association, 2000. This public brochure offers a summary of the common technologies available for desalination.

Clark, J. W., W. Viessman, Jr., and M. J. Hammer. *Water Supply and Pollution Control.* New York: Harper & Row, 1977. This book discusses the growing problem of contamination and available supply of the drinking water resources of the world.

Drew, D. *Karst Processes and Landforms.* New York: MacMillan Education Press, 1985. This is a comprehensive review of the geological conditions that lead to the development of karst terrains.

Fisk, H. N. *Geological Investigation of the Atchafalaya Basin and Problems of the Mississippi River Diversion.* Vicksburg, Va.: U.S. Army Corps of Engineers, Mississippi River Commission, 1952. This U.S. government report is about the major water diversion project along the Mississippi-Atchafalaya river junction, trying to keep water flowing mainly down the Mississippi.

Ford, D., and P. Williams. *Karst Geomorphology and Hydrology.* London: Unwin-Hyman, 1989. This book describes the groundwater system in karst terrains.

Galloway, W. E., and D. K. Hobday. *Terrigineous Clastic Depositional Systems.* New York: Springer-Verlag, 1983. This is an advanced college book on sedimentary systems on the continents including river systems.

Gordon, N. D., T. A. McMahon, and B. L. Finlayson. *Stream Hydrology: An Introduction for Ecologists.* New York: John Wiley & Sons. 1992. This is an elementary book for nonspecialists on the hydrology and dynamics of streams.

Hirshleiffer, J., J. C. de haven, and J. W. Milliman. *Water Supply: Economics, Technology, and Policy.* Chicago: University of Chicago Press, 1960. An in-depth analysis of bringing water to places that lack a reliable supply.

Jennings, J. N. *Karst Geomorphology.* Oxford: Basil Blackwell, 1985. This is a comprehensive treatise on different types of karst landforms.

Kusky, T. M. *Encyclopedia of Earth Science.* New York: Facts On File, 2004. A comprehensive encyclopedia of earth sciences written for college and high school audiences, as well as the general public.

Leopold, L. B. *A View of the River.* Cambridge, Mass.: Harvard University Press, 1994. This is a layman's description of river systems.

Noble, C. C. "The Mississippi River Flood of 1973." In *Geomorphology and Engineering,* edited by D. R. Coates, 79–98. London: Allen & Unwin, 1980. A detailed description of the catastrophic Mississippi River flood of 1973.

Parsons, A. J., and A. D. Abrahams. *Overland Flow: Hydraulics and Erosion Mechanics.* London: University College London Press, 1992. This is a technical book on the flow of water across the land surface.

Ritter, D. F., R. C. Kochel, and J. R. Miller. *Process Geomorphology.* 3d ed. Boston: WCB–McGraw Hill, 1995. This is a comprehensive book describing modern views on geomorphology and river system dynamics.

Rosgen, D. *Applied River Morphology.* Pasoga Springs, Colo.: Wildland Hydrology, 1966. This is an early book describing the main geomorphological features of river systems and how they may impact people.

Schumm, S. A. *The Fluvial System.* New York: Wiley-Interscience: 1977. This is a classic on river systems and the sediments they deposit.

White, W. B. *Geomorphology and Hydrology of Karst Terrains.* Oxford: Oxford University Press, 1988. This technical book describes the main geomorphic features and groundwater flow in karst terrains.

JOURNAL ARTICLES

Alley, W. M., T. E. Reilly, and O. L. Franke. "Sustainability of Ground-Water Resources." *U.S. Geological Survey Circular* 1186 (1999). This 79-page article discusses how long the groundwater resources in the United States might last at current rates of use.

Arnold, J. G., P. J. Boison, and P. C. Patton. "Sawmill Brook: An Example of Rapid Geomorphic Change Related to Urbanization." *Journal of Geology* 90 (1982): 115–166. This article documents the changes in the river dynamics resulting from development and urbanization.

Baker, V. R. "Stream-Channel Responses to Floods, with Examples from Central Texas." *Geological Society of America Bulletin* 88 (1977): 1,057–1,071. This paper documents how increased discharge can change the cross-sectional area of a river.

Belt, C. B., Jr. "The 1973 Flood and Man's Constriction of the Mississippi River." *Science* 189 (1975): 681–684. This classic paper demonstrated how building levees and wing dikes along the Mississippi River has increased the flood levels along the river for specific amounts of water.

Booth, D. B. "Stream Channel Incision Following Drainage Basin Urbanization." *Water Resources Bulletin* 26 (1990): 407–417. This paper shows some responses of the river channel to urbanization.

Collier, M. P., R. H. Webb, and E. D. Andrews. "Experimental Flooding in the Grand Canyon." *Scientific American* (January 1997), 82–89. This is an informal discussion of a test of using regulated floods to try to restore some of the riverbed features of the heavily dammed Colorado River.

Dolan, R., and H. Grant Goodell. "Sinking Cities." *American Scientist* 74 (1986): 38–47. Documentation that some coastal cities, such as New Orleans, are inexorably sinking below sea level.

Hesse, L. W., and W. Sheets. "The Missouri River Hydrosystem." *Fisheries* 18 (1993): 5–14. This is an overview of the Missouri River drainage system.

Holzer, T. L., ed. "Man-Induced Land Subsidence." *Geological Society of America, Reviews in Engineering Geology* 6 (1984): This is a 221-page discussion of human-induced cases of land subsidence, mainly from oil and water extraction from underground sources.

Howard, Arthur D. "Drainage Analysis in Geologic Interpretation: A Summation." *American Association of Petroleum Geologists Bulletin* 51 (1967): 2,246–2,259. This classic paper presents the widely used classification of drainage basin types based on the style of branching of the river networks.

Jacobson, R. B., S. R. Femmer, and R. A. McKennery. "Land Use Changes and the Physical Habitat of Streams: A Review with Emphasis on Studies within the U.S." *Geological Survey Federal-State Cooperative Program, U.S. Geological Survey Circular* 1175 (2001): This is a 63-page technical report summarizing how urbanization is changing the patterns of riverbeds and floods in the United States.

Junk, W. J., P. B. Bayley, and R. E. Sparks. "The Flood Pulse Concept in River-Floodplain Systems." *Canadian Special Publication Fisheries and Aquatic Sciences,* 106 (1989): 110–127. Presents idea that floods are a major spike in activity in controlling the morphology of flood plains.

Leopold, L. B., and M. G. Wolman. "River Channel Patterns—Braided, Meandering, and Straight." *U.S. Geological Survey Professional Paper 282-B* (1957). This classic paper describes straight, meandering, and braided stream patterns and their possible causes.

Maddock, T., Jr. "A Primer on Floodplain Dynamics." *Journal of Soil and Water Conservation* 31 (1976): 44–47. This paper discusses river-floodplain dynamics and their interrelationships.

Pan, Z., M. Segal, and C. Graves. "On the Potential Change in Surface Water Vapor Deposition over the Continental United States Due to Increases in Atmospheric Greenhouse Gases." *Journal of Climate* 19 (2006): 1,576–1,585. This paper describes the so-called atmospheric warming holes that cause the U.S. Midwest, eastern China, and the Amazon Basin to become wetter and slightly cooler while the rest of the planet gets warmer.

Pan, Z., R. W. Arritt, E. S. Takle, et al. "Altered Hydrologic Feedback in a Warming Climate Introduces a 'Warming Hole,'" *Geophysical Research Letters* 31 (2004): L17109, do: 10.10129/2004GLO20528. This paper was the first to describe the atmospheric warming hole that causes the midwestern United States to become wetter and slightly cooler while the rest of the planet gets warmer during global warming.

Solley, W. B., R. R. Pierce, and H. A. Perlman. "Estimated use of water in the United States in 1995." *U.S. Geological Survey Circular* 1200 (1998): This is a 71-page survey of how much water was used for which purposes in the United States in 1995.

U.S. Geological Survey. "Storm and Flood of July 31–August 1, 1976, in the Big Thompson and Cache la Poudre River Basins, Larimer and Weld Counties, Colorado." *U.S. Geological Survey Professional Paper* 1115 (1979): 152. This is a description of the Big Thompson Canyon flood of 1976.

WEB SITES

In the past few years numerous Web sites with information about floods and groundwater hazards have appeared. Most of these Web sites offer free access and include historical information about specific hazards and disasters, real-time monitoring of active floods around the world, and educational material. The sites listed below have interesting information, statistics, and graphics about these hazards. The following list of Web sites is recommended to help enrich the content of this book and make your exploration of floods, groundwater resources and contamination, and subsidence more enjoyable. In addition, any floods or water disasters that occur after this book was published will undoubtedly be discussed on these Web sites, so consulting them can help you keep this book up to date. From these Web sites you will also be able to link to a large variety of hazard-related sites. Every effort has been made to ensure the accuracy of the information provided for these Web sites; however, due to the dynamic nature of the Internet, changes might occur, and any inconvenience is regretted.

Federal Emergency Management Agency (FEMA). The nation's premier emergency management agency, FEMA deals with emergency management and preparation and issues warnings and evacuation orders when disasters appear imminent. FEMA maintains a Web site that is updated at least daily and includes information about hurricanes, floods, fires, national flood insurance, disaster prevention and preparation, and emergency management. The site is divided into national and regional sites. It also contains information on costs of disasters, maps, and directions on how to do business with FEMA. Available online. URL: http://www.fema.gov. Accessed May 23, 2007.

Karst Waters Institute (KWI). A nonprofit institution, the KWI's mission is "to improve the fundamental understanding of karst water systems through sound scientific research and the education of professionals and the public. . . . Institute activities include the initiation, coordination, and conduct of research, the sponsorship of conferences and workshops, and occasional publication of scientific works. KWI supports these activities by acting as a coordinating agency for funding and personnel, but does not supply direct funding or grants to individual researchers." As one way of increasing public awareness of karst and cave protection, KWI publishes a list of the top-10 endangered karst environments in the world. Available online. URL: http://www. karstwaters.org. Accessed December 10, 2007.

National Aeronautics and Space Administration (NASA). Earth scientists around the world use NASA satellite imagery to better understand the causes and effects of natural hazards. NASA's natural hazards page posts many public domain images to help people visualize where and when natural hazards occur and to help mitigate their effects. All images in this section are freely available to the public for reuse or publication. Available online. URL: http://earthobservatory.nasa.gov/NaturalHazards/. Accessed May 23, 2007.

National Weather Service (NWS). The NWS, FEMA, and the Red Cross maintain a Web site dedicated to describing how to prepare for floods, describing floods of various types, giving in-depth descriptions of warnings, and explaining types of home emergency kits that families should keep in their homes. Available online. URL: http://www.nws.noaa.gov/om/brochures/ffbro.htm. Accessed December 10, 2007.

Natural Hazards Observer. This Web site is the online version of the bimonthly periodical of the Natural Hazards Center, *The Natural Hazards Observer.* It covers current disaster issues; new international, national, and local disaster management, mitigation, and education programs; hazards research; political and policy developments; new information sources and Web sites; upcoming conferences; and recent publications. Distributed to more than 15,000 subscribers in the United States and abroad, the Observer focuses online on news regarding human adaptation and response to natural hazards and other catastrophic events and provides a forum for concerned individuals to express opinions and generate new ideas through invited personal articles. Available online. URL: http://www.colorado.edu/hazards/o/. Accessed December 17, 2007.

United States Army Corps of Engineers. The U.S. Army Corps of Engineers has an emergency response unit for responding to environmental, coastal, and other disasters. The Headquarters Office (http://www.usace.army.mil/where.html#Headquarters) is a good place to start a search for any specific problem. Available online. URL: http://www.erdc.usace.army.mil/. Accessed December 17, 2007.

United States Environmental Protection Agency (EPA). The EPA works with other government agencies and private organizations to monitor groundwater quality and contamination, Superfund sites, subsidence and sinkhole hazards, and many other environmental issues. Available online. URL: http://www.epa.gov. Accessed December 10, 2007.

United States Geological Survey (USGS), Hazards Research. This page on the USGS Web site has descriptions of many geological hazards, with specifics on coastal hazards. In the United States each year, natural hazards cause hundreds of deaths and cost tens of billions of dollars in disaster aid, disruption of commerce, and destruction of homes and critical infrastructure. This series of pages was designed to educate citizens, emergency managers, and lawmakers on seven natural hazards facing the nation—earthquakes, floods, hurricanes, landslides, tsunamis, volcanoes, and wildfires—and show how USGS science helps mitigate disasters and build resilient communities. Available online. URL: http://www.usgs.gov/themes/hazard.html. Accessed May 23, 2007.

United States Geological Survey (USGS), Water Resources. The USGS, among other things, monitors weather and streamflow conditions nationwide, as well as groundwater levels. This page on its Web site also contains information on water quality and use and contains maps and charts of water-use-related issues. The site has links to other related Web sites. Available online. URL: http://water.usgs.gov/. Accessed December 10, 2007.

Index

Note: Page numbers in *italic* refer to illustrations, *m* indicates a map, *t* indicates a table.